Hands-On Geography

by
Susan Buckley and Elspeth Leacock

SCHOLASTIC
PROFESSIONAL BOOKS

New York • Toronto • London • Auckland • Sydney

For the dedicated teachers who gave us their love of the world.

The authors wish to thank Donna LaRoche and Marshall Levy, who inspire young geographers at Winn Brook School in Belmont, Massachusetts, and who generously shared with us their classroom experience and geographic wisdom.

Cover design by Vincent Ceci
Cover illustration by Joseph O'Rourke
Book design by Nancy Metcalf, Intergraphics
Book illustrations by David De Gasperis

ISBN 0-590-49351-5

Contents

continued

continued

A LONG WAY: Using Distance Scales

WHAT'S WHAT: Using Symbols

LAND AND WATER: Learning About Physical Geography

IT'S RAINING, IT'S POURING: Learning About Climate

OUR TOWN: Making A Model Community

GETTING DOWN TO BUSINESS: Learning About Economic Geography

LONG, LONG AGO: Learning About Historical Geography

DREAMTOWN: Learning About Urban Geography

Reproducibles　　81
....

Introduction

A ll children are born with an innate curiosity about the world around them. They love to explore and find out—to question and learn. We don't usually refer to children as *geographers*, but in fact that is what they are—*young geographers*. They do exactly what geographers do. They look at the world and ask questions about who does what, where, and why. They are curious about why the world looks as it does and how that affects their lives. That is the work of geographers.

The word *geography*, which comes from the Greek words which mean "to write about the Earth," should convey a sense of the excitement and adventure of discovery. Today, American children have easy access to more geographic information than ever before. They are exposed to images of all of the world's landforms, climates, cultures, economies, and politics—from times past, present, and future. Through television, movies, books, and magazines they have seen the Arctic and the Sahara, the people of the rain forest and the tundra, hunter-gatherer societies, as well as agrarian, mercantile, and industrial societies. This is the stuff of excitement and discovery.

If we as educators can bring this excitement to the classroom, we will give our children a priceless gift. We will open their eyes to a world that is theirs to discover and explore. We hope that *Hands-On Geography* will help you bring that excitement to your children.

Hands-On Learning

As its title promises, *Hands-On Geography* gives primary children practical experience with maps, the geographer's most basic tool, and with many related geographical ideas.

This book is divided into two parts: **Getting Started** and **Being a Geographer**. In each, activities are grouped by geographic topic (e.g., directions, climate, etc.). For early-primary classrooms where children are just beginning to learn about maps and geography, the activities found in **Getting Started** can be used to introduce children to new ways to view the world around them. In the process, they will learn the basic components and concepts found on maps and even make their own maps. In **Being a Geographer,** children will have opportunities to learn more sophisticated skills and apply a higher order of geographic thinking. These activities will help develop more advanced map skills and concepts of cultural, economic, historical, and urban geography—all on a level appropriate for primary classrooms. In many activities in both parts of the book, suggestions are made for how to link the study of geography with other areas of the curriculum.

A full-color, two-sided poster and more than forty reproducibles are also parts of **Hands-On Geography**. The poster features an imaginary town called *Geotown* which children can use to practice their newfound geographic skills. The reproducibles, found at the back of this book, are an integral part of many of the activities.

Geography's Themes

Hands-On Geography is based on the principle that geography is about looking—looking at the world in a certain way. In the 1980s, thanks to a program spearheaded by the National Geographic Society, geographers and teachers of children from kindergarten through grade twelve worked together to develop a clear framework that makes it easier for us to organize what we see when we look at the world as geographers. The framework is based on these five themes:

Location: Geographers—whether children or professors—want to know where people and places are on Earth, their exact location, and their location relative to other people or places.

Place: All places have special features that distinguish them from other places. Some of these characteristics are physical, like rain forests, sandy beaches, or snowy mountains. Others are human-made, like crowded cities, small towns,churches, or skyscrapers.

Human-Environment Interactions: Geographers look at ways in which humans affect the environment and how the environment affects humans.

Movement: The movement of people, goods, and ideas across the earth is also part of geography. What happened when pioneers settled on the Great Plains? How does an apple get from Washington State to New York? What effect does American music have on the world? All of these questions concern geography.

Regions: Geographers study Earth's regions, whether they are political regions, like nations or states; language regions, like the Hispanic world; or landform regions, like the Rocky Mountains.

Understanding that all of these big ideas are part of geography helps you make your geography teaching more relevant, more interesting, and much more enjoyable for your young geographers.

GETTING STARTED

The activities found in **Getting Started** have two aims: first, to support you in helping children to see the world around them as geographers, and second, to develop in children an understanding of the basic principles on which maps are based.

Getting Started is divided into eight sections, each with a set of activities focusing on one topic. The activities are designed to let children explore, practice, and play with ideas. Some of these ideas are as simple as looking at the place in which they live in terms of the shape of its land. Others are as complex as examining the relationship between real distance on Earth and scale distance on a map. By making all of these ideas accessible to children through simple activities and manipulatives, we hope that we have given you tools to enrich the creative teaching that you already do.

PICTURING PLACES
Learning To Look

To one degree or another, we all take for granted the place where we live. Few of us consistently *read* the landscape by observing or analyzing the physical and human characteristics of that place. Like all other people, children often look at, but do not really *see* what is around them. This awareness of place can be an underlying theme woven into activities and discussion throughout the year. The activities that follow are designed to help children develop a greater awareness of their own environment, to see places familiar to them in a new light with the eyes of a geographer, and to discuss the places, using the terminology common to all geographers.

Creating A Geography Word Web

A word web can help you find out how well your children see their surroundings and give them a sense that they already know a lot about the place where they live. Make a word web based on all of the words children suggest to describe the physical and human characteristics of their community.

What To Do

1. Write the name of their community in a circle on the board and invite children to tell you about this *place* where they live. Encourage the children to tell you any names for the neighborhood or parts of their community and anything else they can think of that would describe it. Guide the discussion toward physical characteristics (hilly, flat, or green), toward climate (hot, windy, or snowy), and toward land or water features (mountains, lakes, or oceans).

2. Write all of their suggestions on the board around the central circle, without taking the time to organize the ideas at this time.

3. You may want to use some mental mapping or guided imagery to help children focus on geographic features. For example, you might ask the children to close their eyes and imagine what would happen if they took away all the buildings and streets in their neighborhood. What would the land look like underneath? Would it still be hilly or flat? Would the river, lake, or ocean still be there? In other words, help them sort out the difference between physical geography (the natural features of the land, such as landforms and climate), and cultural or human geography (people—where and how they live and what they have made).

4. If children don't name certain significant physical features that they should be aware of, such as a river running through town, make your own contributions to the word web. The object here is not to teach children new terms, but to include as many characteristics as possible.

5. Help the children categorize these place descriptors on chart paper. For example, they can group all of the landform words on one chart and climate words on another. Children can add to and use these word banks throughout the year. You can use them as the basis of spelling lists, sentence starters, and thinking-skill activities like categorizing or comparing.

6. Point out to the class that they already know a lot about the place where they live, but they are going to set out on an adventure to find out even more about it. Tell the class that they are going to be *geographers*. Help them to understand that geographers are people who learn about places—what the places look like and what people do there. Dramatize this new word in such a way that the children feel that being a geographer is something very special indeed!

Take the children on a short walk outside to sharpen their skills of observation, speculation, analysis, and evaluation. These skills are the basis for good thinking at any age.

Materials Needed

1. Plastic gallon jug of water

2. Sketch pads (made from pieces of corrugated board or cardboard)

3. Pencils

What To Do

1. Invite the class to go on a "geography walk" with you. Now that they know the word *geography*, ask them what they think a geography walk might be. Help them understand that they are going to look at a familiar place through the eyes of geographers.

2. When you get outside, invite the children to tell you what they see. You may want to make notes on the children's comments for later discussion. Ask them what each place looks like. Questions like the following can prompt the children to see through the eyes of geographers:

○ Is the land absolutely flat or does it slope?

○ When it rains, which way does the water flow? (Pour water from the jug onto the street near the curb to demonstrate the slope.) Is the water moving? Which way is it going? Which way is downhill? Which way is uphill?

○ Is there a drain? Where do you think the water goes from there? Is there a river or lake or ocean nearby? Where is it? Could the water run into that?

○ Are there mountains or hills near enough to see? What do they look like? Which way are they?

○ What kinds of plants grow in the neighborhood? Can you see any parks?

○ What kind of animals are in your neighborhood? What do you think the animals eat for food?

○ What have people built in the neighborhood? What buildings can you name? What do the streets and roads look like?

3. Back in the classroom, help children analyze what they saw. One way to do this is to make two charts. On one, children can draw pictures and dictate words describing things people have made. The second chart can show natural features of the neighborhood.

4. Children have the innate ability to evaluate land use. Invite them to tell what they think about what they saw. Did they see places to live and places to shop? Are the places pretty? Busy? Crowded? Are there places to play and walk, or is all of the land filled up with other things?

Across The Curriculum

Linking Art And Geography

Before the geography walk described above, provide each child with a sketch pad made out of one sheet of paper paper-clipped onto a piece of corrugated board or cardboard. Ask each child to make a sketch of something about the land that they want to remember. Back in the classroom offer opportunities to share what they drew and why. Drawings can be compiled into a big book or hung on a bulletin board for all to see.

Making A Big Book Of Places

Materials Needed

1. Magazines, calendars, travel brochures
2. Scissors
3. Paste

Before Starting

Encourage the children and their families to help you gather a large collection of consumable sources that contain pictures of places. Travel magazines and brochures, state magazines, and old calendars are good sources. Local travel agencies may be helpful in supplying materials. Also, make a blank big book titled *Our Big Book of Places*.

What To Do

1. Invite the children to use the picture collection to identify and cut out pictures of places.

2. Help the children categorize the pictures into as many groupings as are necessary. At this point you may need to give children some new vocabulary to describe physical features that they have never seen before, like mountains or deserts. If possible, have available a children's reference book like *Geography from A to Z* by Jack Knowlton (HarperCollins) from which you can read aloud and which you can use to show children descriptions of various geographic features.

3. Be sure the children understand that a picture of a place can be grouped in different ways. A city scene in winter, for example, could be in a grouping called "Places with Lots of People"

or in one titled "Places That Are Cold." Help children decide on the categories that they want to include in their book and encourage them to arrange the pictures accordingly.

4. After the children have pasted the pictures onto the pages of the big book, you can use it to talk about places in various ways. For example, invite the children to find pictures in the book that look like the place where they live, or talk about what it might be like to live in a place different from theirs.

Across The Curriculum

Linking Writing And Geography

The big book can also be the basis of writing activities. Children can pick a picture and tell why they would or would not like to live there, what they'd do there, and who they might meet there.

Linking Literature And Geography

Throughout the year, help children to become aware of the verbal and visual descriptions of places in the books they read and hear read. Turn the children into "geography detectives" as they look and listen for clues about the setting, the climate, the landforms, or other geographic information. Books like *The Little House* by Virginia Lee (Houghton Mifflin) are especially rich sources of geographic information. In this book, children can trace changes in the land and the seasons, as well as see the striking transformation of the human-made environment around the house. You can use Reproducible 42 (p. 122) to make blue ribbons to award outstanding detectives.

A VIEW FROM ABOVE
Introducing Perspective

Maps are one of the geographer's most useful tools. All maps, whether simple picture maps or complex topographic maps, are views of a place as seen from above. An understanding of this perspective—a view from above—is an essential first step in seeing a map as a special kind of picture of a place.

Viewing Things From Eye Level And Above

The ease with which your children grasp the concept of perspective will depend on their developmental level. The more concrete their thinking, the more physically active you will want to make the activities about perspective. In this activity, the children will look at and compare a familiar object from two different viewpoints.

Materials Needed

1. Reproducible 1 (p. 81)

2. Apple's (one per small group)

3. Portable objects such as plants and small boxes

What To Do

1. Place the real apples on tables and ask the children to view them at eye level, that is, at the level of the table. Then place the apples on the floor and invite the children to stand up and look directly down on them. This physical action of looking at eye level and looking down is especially important for younger children who may have trouble making this perceptual connection. Encourage children to discuss how the apple looks the same and how it looks different in the two views. To reinforce the connection, repeat

this with a variety of classroom objects, such as a plant or small box.

2. Display one copy of Reproducible 1 and point to a view of the apple. Ask children what this is, then help them match it to the other view of an apple. Place the real apple at eye level and on the floor and have children match the picture to the correct view. Help children understand that "an apple is an apple is an apple" no matter how they look at it.

3. Present the remaining sets of cards, one set at a time, and have the children identify the perspective in each, using the terms *eye level* or *from above* to describe each viewpoint.

4. Distribute a copy of Reproducible 1 to each of the children. After they have cut out all eight picture cards, they can select pairs of pictures to color. However, remind the children that if the fish, for example, are yellow in the eye level picture, they should also be yellow when seen from above. Then, invite them to sort the pictures in two ways. First, they can sort them in pairs of matching objects and second, in sets of pictures seen from eye level and those seen from above. At another time, you can play a game by distributing one card to each of eight children. A child with the apple seen from above will find a child with the apple seen at eye level, and so on.

Across The Curriculum

Linking Math And Geography

When the children are finished observing the apple, you may want to use it for a simple math lesson on fractions. Cut the apple in half and ask the children if the pieces are the same size. Ask them how they can describe the pieces after they have been cut. Continue cutting and identifying the parts until the apple is in bite-size pieces. Then eat them!

Linking Literature And Geography

To give a different perspective on perspective (so to speak), read *Ben's Dream* by Chris Van Allsburg (Houghton Mifflin) to the children. It presents a small child's view of very large monuments.

Linking Art And Geography

Make available to the children a number of objects to draw from above. After all the pictures have been drawn, one child at a time can select a picture from the stack and match it with the object itself.

Viewing Places From Above

Materials Needed

1. Reproducible 2 (p. 82)

2. Scissors

What To Do

1. Ask children to imagine that they are birds flying in the sky above their school's neighborhood. Help them visualize the scene they would see from above—the buildings, people, trees, and so on. Encourage the children to compare this bird's-eye view to the way they saw the apple when they stood over it.

2. You can do the same activities with Reproducible 2 that you did with Reproducible 1.

3. Divide children into groups of four or five. Ask for a volunteer to act as the announcer

who will choose and describe a card, such as "the pet store seen from above." Each child in the group who has that card should hold it up. Allow the children to take turns being the announcer with the previous caller rejoining the group each time.

Across The Curriculum

Linking Writing and Geography

Children can dictate a story to you or write their own scribble stories about what they see from above on a flying trip—either in an airplane or as imaginary character like Peter Pan or Aladdin.

Picturing Places

The picture of Geotown on the Poster (Side 1, Band A) will help you guide your children along the steps necessary to move from seeing an actual place, to seeing a picture of it, and later to seeing a map as an abstract representation of that real place.

Materials Needed

1. Poster (Side 1, Band A)

2. Reproducible 2 (p. 82)

3. Drawing paper

4. Tempera paints, colored pencils, crayons

5. Photographs of your school

Before Starting

Take or obtain several photographs of your school.

What To Do

1. To reinforce children's connections between places and pictures, invite them to talk about their favorite place in their neighborhood. Encourage detailed descriptions so that the children form good mental pictures of the place they have chosen. Then make drawing materials available and invite the children to create pictures of their places. Allow each child to tell you about his or her picture. Ask whether it is a view from eye level or from above.

2. Show the children the photographs of their school and talk about them as pictures of a real place that they know. Discuss with the class other kinds of pictures of places the children have seen. Then introduce them to the top band of the Poster, Side 1 (you may want to cover up the middle and bottom bands) explaining that this is also a picture of a place—a street in a place called Geotown.

3. For reinforcement, distribute copies of Reproducible 2. Have children identify the four left hand pictures as places seen from eye level. Let children arrange the pictures on another sheet of paper to create street scenes. (Save the right hand pictures—the views from above—for the next activity.)

Recognizing Geotown From Above

Materials Needed

1. Poster (Side 1, Band B)

2. Reproducible 2 (p. 82)

Note: The middle band of Poster (Side 1) is a kind of picture map—a halfway step between a picture and a map. For this activity, refer to it as a *picture*, since *map* is better defined when using the actual map.

What To Do

1. Show children the middle band of the poster and help them see that it is a view of Geotown from above. Help children find the same street in the pictures in both the top and middle bands. (You might point to the church in both pictures.) Have children explain the ways the two pictures differ and how they are alike.

2. Now let children use the views from above on Reproducible 2 to match the street scenes they created earlier.

Across The Curriculum

Linking Literature And Geography

As the Crow Flies by Gail Hartman (Bradbury Press) is a charming picture book that works perfectly as a conclusion to this section. Harvey Stevenson's drawings illustrate the views seen from the different perspectives of eagle, rabbit, crow, horse, and seagull. Together they create a picture map.

WHICH WAY?
Introducing Directions

Differentiating right from left often confuses children, and acquiring the skill can be challenging. These exercises are designed to help children practice identifying right and left in a playful atmosphere. Developing this skill—necessary for everything from knitting to space travel—helps prepare children for using the cardinal directions of north, south, east, and west.

Recognizing Right And Left

Materials Needed

Red yarn or washable marker

What To Do

1. Identify each students' right hand by tying a bit of red yarn loosely around their wrists or marking their hands with red "R's". Explain that "red" or "R" stands for "right". An interesting play on words that helps many children learn the difference is "This is your right hand and this one is left." (as in left over).

2. Play a game of Simon Says using the commands "Simon says hold up your right hand." "Simon says hold up your left hand." After children practice left/right recognition this way, move to more challenging commands such as "Simon says turn right." "Simon says turn left." "Now turn left." In this game children are not eliminated for turning in the wrong direction, but for obeying a command without the requisite "Simon says...." This gives the children more practice and removes some of the onus from mixing up the directions. You may also want to allow

children who have been eliminated to take turns giving the commands.

Across The Curriculum

Linking Math and Geography

Let "Simon" clap his or her hands for the number of steps the players are to take.

Practicing Right And Left

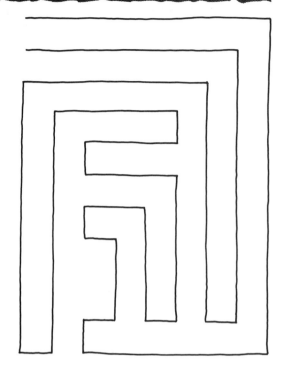

Materials Needed

1. Reproducible 42 (p. 122)

2. Chalk or tape

3. Stop watch

4. Crayons (blue)

Before Starting

1. Make two ribbons using Reproducible 42 and color them blue.

2. Use chalk to lay out a race course on the ground with lots of 90° angles at which one can turn in only one direction. Angles should zigzag in both left and right directions (see diagram). Note: This game is best played outside in the school yard, although you can adapt it, with a great deal of tape, on an inside floor.

3. Create a score sheet with three columns. In the first column, write each child's name. Write "Time" and "Number of Red Lights" over the second and third columns.

What To Do

1. Allow the children to run the course, one at a time. Each time a runner reaches a turn, he or she must call "left" if turning left, or "right" if turning right. If the runner identifies the correct direction, the group will call "green light." If the runner is incorrect, the group will call "red light," and he or she can try again. After all the children have had a turn, use the stop watch and allow each child to run the course again—this time being timed. There can be two winners, the runner with the fewest red lights and the runner with the fastest time. Award the winners with blue ribbons or some other special acknowledgement.

2. To go a step further, have the children share how they remember which is their right hand and which is their left. They might want to research by asking their parents or friends to describe how they learned or how they remember which is right. You might also tally the number of left-handed and right-handed people in the class, remembering to include yourself.

Across The Curriculum

Linking Math And Geography

Ask children to count how many times they turn right and how many times they turn left on their way to school. Make a trip through the school building to the gym, for example, and have children tally the turns. This might work best if children work in pairs, with one child doing the tallying.

Expanding The Concept Of Direction

When you feel that children have a solid grounding in distinguishing left from right, introduce the concept of direction itself. At the same time, broaden the directions that the children use to include up/down, back/front, above/below, and so on. Eventually, the children will be able to transpose these into an understanding of north, south, east, and west.

What To Do

1. Write the word *direction* on the board. Then— with your back turned to the children— extend your right arm to your right while pointing your finger in that direction. Ask the children which way you are pointing. Explain that the word *direction* is another way of saying "which way." Ask, "Which way am I pointing?" Then ask, "In which direction am I pointing?"

2. You can practice right/left, up/down, back/front, and above/below with the children by playing a version of Simon Says which will help them internalize the concept of directions. Allow the children to take turns directing you by saying their own names and a

direction. For example, "Lucy says the direction is right."

Across The Curriculum

Linking Literature And Geography

The classic *The Red Balloon* by A. Larorisse (Doubleday) offers an opportunity for children to practice using simple directions. Children can retell the story in terms of the balloon's direction—up, down, left, right, and so on.

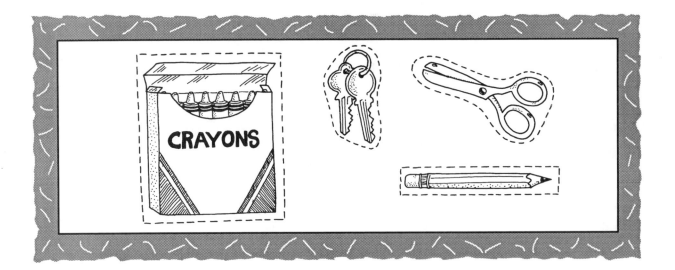

HOW BIG?
Introducing Scale

All children know that there are small versions of large things—model cars, dolls, doll houses. In fact, children themselves are small versions of large adults. Although children do not associate the word *scale* to a system of measuring anything but weight, they do understand the basic concept of small/large scale. The object of the following activities is to help children identify small-scale and full-scale depictions of the same place, to better understand that maps are small-scale pictures of full-scale places.

Distinguishing Between Full Scale And Small Scale

Materials Needed

1. Reproducible 3 (p.83)

2. Scissors

What To Do

1. Call on children's existing knowledge of scale, by asking if anyone has stuffed animals, dolls, soldiers, or toy trucks at home. Have the children describe the differences between a real home and a doll house, a real soldier and a toy soldier, and a real truck and a toy truck. Size should come up again and again.

2. Hold up Reproducible 3 and point out the two pictures of crayon boxes. Ask children to tell you the difference between the two. Then have children cut out the pictures on their reproducible. Invite them to hold up the large-sized picture of crayons and then the small-sized picture. Continue in the same way with each pair of pictures.

3. You may want to introduce the word *scale* at this point. Ask the class to tell you everything they know about scales. They will undoubtedly be familiar with scales that weigh

people and objects. Explain that scales can measure many things—weight, size, etc. Point out that a picture is a small-scale version of the real scene or people, which are full-scale size. A model train is a small-scale version of a full-scale train which transports goods and people.

4. Invite the children to bring an interesting scale model from home to share with the class. Allow each child to describe the differences between the small- and large-scale things.

Creating Full And Small Scale Drawings

To start with the closest reality they know, children can use themselves as the subject of scale drawings.

Materials Needed

1. Large (body-size) sheets of paper
2. 8 1/2 by 11 sheets of paper
3. Scissors
4. Crayons or markers

Before Starting

Cut rectangles of paper slightly larger than the tallest child in your class. Make one rectangle for each child, with a few extras in case you need them. You may want to have teacher's aides or parents help with this project.

What To Do

1. While each child in turn lies on a piece of

paper, have someone trace the child's outline with a marker.

2. Allow children to color their pictures. Then ask them what scale these drawings are. (*Answer: Full-scale*)

3. Ask children to make small-scale drawings of themselves. By giving them smaller-sized pieces of paper, you will remind them of the comparative sizes.

4. Display the full- and small-scaled pictures along the school hallway or in the classroom. The class can make up a title for the display, using the word *scale* if you have introduced it.

Across The Curriculum

Linking Science And Geography

Use the full-scale drawings to practice naming body parts. You can even combine this with practice in directions by asking children silly, but effective, questions such as, "Where are your shoulders? Is your head above or below your shoulders?" Avoid asking any questions about right and left unless children are holding their drawings in front of and facing away from them.

Using Grid Paper To Create Small Scale Drawings

This variation on scale drawings uses a grid to teach children that a small-scale drawing can be a precise version of a full-scale object.

Materials Needed

1. Reproducible 4 (p.84)
2. Pencils

3. Assorted blocks (large enough to cover more than one grid square)

What To Do

1. Allow children each to choose a block to reproduce. Explain that they are going to make full-scale drawings of their blocks. Distribute copies of Reproducible 4 and have children place their blocks anyplace they want on the large grid and trace around the blocks.

2. Point out the smaller grid and ask children how they could use the numbers on the two grids to help them make small-scale drawings of their blocks. Lead them to understand that they can copy in each small box what they see in the comparable larger box.

3. After the children make small-scale drawings of their blocks, ask them to tell you how they did it. Then point to a grid box on a full-scale drawing and ask a child to identify the same box on the small-scale drawing.

4. Repeat the exercise having the children trace their hands on the large boxes, and draw a small-scale hand in the small boxes.

Creating A Model Of The Classroom

Materials Needed

1. Reproducible 5 (p. 85)

2. Large sheet of paper

3. Paste

Before Starting

1. Make a floor plan of the classroom by measuring or estimating the length and width of the classroom.

2. On the large sheet of paper, draw the classroom using the scale: 1 inch represents 1 foot. For example, if your classroom measures 22 feet by 19 feet, draw a rectangle that is 22 inches by 19 inches. Adding some details (door, windows, or furniture), will help the children recognize the space. (Adding a grid of 1 inch squares on the plan will help you use it for location questions later.)

What To Do

1. Using copies of Reproducible 5, have children make model desks to represent each desk in the room. (If children's fine motor skills make this a problem, use small blocks or sugar cubes instead.) Children can identify their desks by writing their names or drawing pictures on them. Note: Children will find it easier to write on their desk patterns before they glue the flaps.

2. Help the children arrange their desks on the floor plan. Using imagination and the right art supplies, the children may want to add scale models of people, plants, and other objects to the model. Be sure children see this model as a small-scale representation of the full-scale classroom.

3. Use the model to compare eye level and above viewpoints and to practice directions. For example, you might ask questions like, "Is the bookcase on the right or the left side of the door?" If you have drawn a grid on the floor plan, ask the children questions about absolute (exact) and relative (in relation to something else) locations. For example, you could have the children identify the exact grid box in which their desks appear (the absolute location). Then ask the children questions such as, "Is the desk next to the window?" (relative location).

4. You can use the model to help children become aware that there are often reasons for location. Ask children to speculate on why

they think the classroom is arranged as it is. For example, if you have put plants and windows on your model, point to them and ask children why the plants are near the windows. You may also want to use the model to allow children to discuss the pros and cons of other ways to arrange the classroom. Save this classroom model for use in later activities.

Relating A Globe To The Earth

Once children feel comfortable relating small-scale models to their larger-scale counterparts, they are ready to make the leap to seeing a globe as a model of the Earth.

Materials Needed
....

1. Globes

2. Satellite photograph of the Earth

What To Do
....

1. If possible, begin by showing children a satellite photograph of the Earth to reinforce its roundness. Ask the children to identify what is in the picture. Tell children that the Earth is sometimes called "the big blue marble" and ask them to speculate about reasons for this.

2. Then present the globe and ask children what they think this is. Let them discuss it as a model or small-scale version of the Earth. If you have a good satellite photograph on which you can identify a continent, point out the shape in the photograph and ask children to try finding something that same shape on the globe.

3. Tell the children that every spot on the Earth is covered with one of two things. Ask them to guess what they are. (land or water). Let volunteers identify the land and water areas in general terms and estimate which covers more of the Earth. (Three-fourths of the Earth is covered by water.)

4. Encourage children to examine and play with the globe as much as they wish. If you have several globes, you can give smaller groups the chance to work more closely with the globes. Help them locate places that they want to find—their state, the country they or their families emigrated from, places they have heard about, and so on.

HOW FAR?
Thinking About Distance

The ability to measure distance has been a critical skill to survival for so long that one cannot imagine a culture without it. The geographer uses distance to define location, characteristics of a place, relationships within places, movement, and regions. These activities will help children understand some of the many ways to think about and calculate distance in a place.

Calculating Relative Distance

Materials Needed

Classroom model (from activity on p. 22-23)

What To Do

1. Play a near/far game asking the children to locate people or objects in the classroom by their relative location. Model the game by saying "I am thinking about someone in our class. Who is it?" When the children suggest names, say "nearer to you" or "farther from you" to help them eventually locate the person. Continue using near/far location words until the children can guess the name of the person. Once the children understand the game, they can take turns being the locator.

2. Have the children identify objects that are near or far from them in the classroom using terms like *nearer* or *farther*. You can do similar exercises with the model classroom, reminding the children that the relative distances and locations in the real classroom are reflected in the model classroom.

3. Children might like to play a version of Blind Man's Bluff in the classroom. They can direct

the blindfolded player to a predetermined spot using distance and direction words like, *near/far, left/right, ahead/behind*, and so on.

Across The Curriculum

Linking Language And Geography

Discuss with the children how words like *near* or *far* help us communicate distance and location. Talk about ways these words would help a blind person know about distance and location. Ask children who speak other languages to share with their classmates the words that they use to communicate distance and location. If you or anyone in the school knows sign language, add this language to the discussion.

Walking Near And Far In Geotown

In preparation for using a distance scale on a map, children can learn to count blocks and use other means of calculating relative distance on a picture map.

Materials Needed

1. Poster (Side 1, Band B)
2. Small doll or toy model of a person

What To Do

1. Gather children around the Poster (Side 1, Band B) and tell them that they are going to take a walk in Geotown. Place your index and third fingers or a small model in front of a

building on the picture map in the middle band. Identify the building with the children, and "walk" your fingers or the model to another building one block away. Have the children volunteer the different ways they could say how far you went (by the number of streets you crossed, by buildings you passed, by how long it took, and so on). This will work best if you make your trip in easily countable blocks on the picture map.

2. Now make two trips to two different locations, still using Band B, and ask children on which "trip" you walked farther. Let children make their own trips on the map, announcing (or having classmates tell) which is farther.

3. Set up hypothetical situations in which someone wants to find the shortest route from one site to another. For example, "Sally has to go from her house to the fountain in the shortest time possible."

Determining The Best Route

Materials Needed

1. Reproducible 6 (p. 86)
2. Scissors
3. Paste
4. Crayons or colored pencils

What To Do

1. Distribute one copy of Reproducible 6 to each child to color, cut out, and assemble one figure. Then read them the following story:

A Day with Aunt Tilly

It is a special day for Georgia. Today, her Aunt Tilly is going to take her wherever she wants to go. Georgia wants to do so many things that she decided to make a list. Here is Georgia's list:

> Aunt Tilly's house
>
> The pet store
>
> The Geotown museum
>
> The park
>
> The library

When Aunt Tilly saw this list, she thought, "I'd better plan this day or my feet are going to quit before the trip is done. I know," thought Tilly, "we'll visit the place farthest away, first. We'll go to my house last, at the end of the day when my feet are too tired to go any further."

2. Repeat aloud the places on Georgia's list and write them on the board in a numbered list. Help the children look at the picture map on the reproducible to decide where they should start, where they should go next, and where they should end the trip. Have them move their figures from one place to the next on their picture map, marking the number of each stop at the correct place.

3. Allow time for learning partners to plan other trips using the maps. Have them label or color on the picture map the places they would like to visit. They can take turns planning the stops and determining the best route. They can draw their routes, using different colors.

Across The Curriculum

Linking History, Math And Geography

Beginning in ancient times, people have devised many different ways of measuring. Ask the children how they might determine size without using a ruler. Share with them some of the ways people used their bodies to measure size and distance long ago. For example, the ancient Egyptians used the *cubit*. That is the distance from the elbow to the tip of the middle finger. Cloth was often measured in *yards*. A yard was the length from a person's nose to the fingertip of his or her outstretched arm. Smaller objects were measured in *spans* or the distance from the top of the small finger to the thumb of an outstretched hand. Even today, horses are measured in *hands*. A hand is the height of a palm. You might have the children measure the distance from one site to another in the school without any standard measuring tools. Encourage children to share their ideas.

WHAT IS IT?
Introducing Symbols

Although children may not be familiar with the term *symbol*, they unconsciously interpret symbols everyday-from the letters and words on a page to the traffic lights they obey on the way to school. By analyzing what they already know, children can expand their understanding and create their own symbol systems.

Developing The Concept Of Symbol

Materials Needed

1. Reproducible 7 (p. 87)

2. Red and green crayons

Before Starting

Cut (but do not color) a set of cards from Reproducible 7 for demonstration purposes.

Note: You may want to have children work in small groups for this exercise, so that they can easily pool their knowledge of symbols.

What To Do

1. Hold up one of the traffic light pictures (from the demonstration pack) and have the groups locate the two traffic lights on their copies of the reproducible. Ask, "If you wanted to cross the street and the traffic light looked like this, what would you do?"

2. Encourage the children to discuss the problem they would face if traffic lights had no colors. Let the children tell what colors the traffic lights should be and then ask them to color in

the top light red on one picture and the bottom light green on the other. Ask them to tell you what red and green represent. Help them see that the colors alone convey important information, but be sure that they understand that the position of the light is also a factor.

3. Have children work together to identify each of the other symbols on the reproducible and tell what each means to them. Explain that all these drawings are symbols and develop an acceptable definition for the word *symbol* with the class. (A color or a simple picture that stands for an idea or a thing.) Ask children to name other symbols that they know.

Matching Pictures With Symbols

Materials Needed

1. Reproducible 8 (p. 88)

2. Scissors

3. Crayons

Note: Depending on the motor skills of your children, this activity can be done by having children cut out and pair the cards, or by having them draw lines to match the symbols to the pictures.

What To Do

1. Distribute a copy of Reproducible 8 to each child. Have the children find the picture of the house, and then the symbol for a house. Ask them to tell you how and why they matched up the two. Repeat this with the other pairs.

2. Encourage the children to discuss the differences between the pictures and the symbols. Help them understand that, visually, these symbols are greatly simplified renderings of the pictures.

3. So that children understand that there is not one universal symbol for something, ask them to create their own symbols for a house. Do the same with a park, train tracks, and bridge.

Across The Curriculum

Linking Writing And Geography

Children can create a set of symbols for places to which they go (e.g., school, home, church, or movies). Then they can make up story sentences of words and pictures. For example, a child might say, "I am going to the park (holding up park symbol) after I leave school (holding up school symbol)."

Linking Visual Literacy And Geography

For homework have the children look in magazines, newspapers, or labels, find a symbol and cut it out or copy it on a piece of paper. If the children need help from their parents or guardians, you could send home the Caregiver Letter on Reproducible 41 (p. 121). After you have collected the symbols, have the class define each one. Mount them with their explanations on the same sheet and place the sheets in a binder. You can title the book *Symbol Dictionary* or *Pictionary*. Have the children add to it as they learn new symbols. Children might also categorize the symbols into groupings like sports, safety, transportation, and so on.

HOT OR COLD?
Thinking About The Seasons

In looking at pictures for seasonal clues, the children will not only learn about the seasons, they will learn how to look at pictures for geographic information. Geographers call this "reading the landscape."

Recognizing The Season In Geotown

Materials Needed

Poster (Side 1, Bands A and B)

What To Do

1. Have the children look at the pictures of Geotown on the top two bands of the Poster (Side 1) and describe the place. Encourage the children to describe as many different places as they can, using the language and observation skills they've learned in the previous activities.

2. Then have children focus on the seasonal clues in the pictures. Ask them what time of year they think it is in Geotown in Band A. Some questions for them to consider are: "Is Geotown at the North Pole?" "Is it in the jungle?" "Is it in the desert?" and "Is it a place like our town?" Be sure to ask the children how they know the answers to these questions. Ask them what they think the weather is like in Geotown in Band B and what clue they can find to help them decide (The trees have no leaves.)

Across The Curriculum

Linking Writing And Geography

Have the children cut pictures out of magazines and old calendars that depict different seasons.

and old calendars that depict different seasons. Have them identify the season and then describe all of the seasonal clues they found in their pictures. Write the words they use on the board or on chart paper under the headings "Summer," "Winter," "Fall," and "Spring." Compare and discuss the word lists. Then have children write or dictate sentences using the words. They can illustrate their sentences with drawings of the seasons.

Recognizing The Signs Of The Season

Materials Needed

1. Reproducibles 9 (p. 89), 10 (p. 90), and 11 (p. 91)

2. Chart paper or board

3. Scissors

4. Crayons

5. Paste

What To Do

1. Have students work in small groups to name a season and talk about what they like or don't like about the weather during that time. Ask them what they like to do during that season and what kinds of clothes they wear and why.

2. On the board or on chart paper, write the name of each season in separate circles. Create word webs with the children for characteristics of each season in their area. Use the word webs to discuss the differences between one season and another. Encourage children to share what they know about seasonal weather differences in other parts of the country or the world.

3. Distribute Reproducibles 9 and 10 and ask children what time of year might be shown in each of the four pictures, articulating the reasons for their choices. Let children color in each picture.

4. After the children color and cut out the figures on Reproducible 11, allow them to arrange and paste down the people and objects on appropriate scenes.

Across The Curriculum

Linking Literature and Geography

The picture book, *The Winter Duckling* by Keith Polette (Milliken), tells of a duck's adventure in winter. Have the children imagine and describe a duck's adventure in other seasons as well.

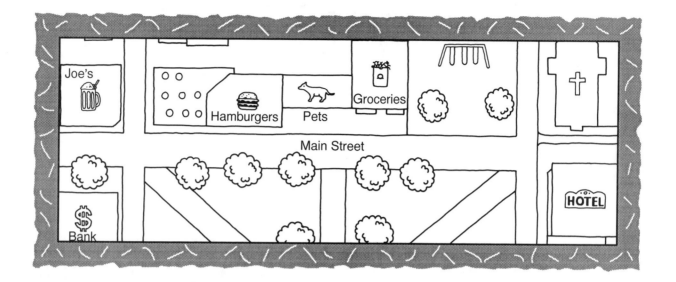

MAP TIME
Putting It All Together On A Map

Maps are geographic pictures of places. Although there is much more to geography than maps, maps are a good way for young children to focus on the characteristics of a place, which is the beginning of geographic inquiry. Now that your children have honed their map skills in the preceding activities, these exercises will help them to put what they have learned about location, directions, distance, scale, and symbols into practice.

Connecting Pictures To Maps

The three views of Geotown on the Poster, (Side 1) offer an opportunity for you to help the children synthesize their learning and put it all together on a map. By contrasting and comparing parallel details in the three views, they can themselves define what a map is and how to use it.

Materials Needed

Poster (Side 1; Bands A, B, and C)

What To Do

1. Using Poster (Side 1), review with the children the pictures of Geotown in the top band (which is seen from eye level) and the middle band (which is seen from above). Have the children compare and point out specific details common and different to both. Reinforce the understanding that the top and middle bands show the same place in different ways.

2. Now focus children's attention on the bottom band, the picture map of Geotown. Tell them that this is another picture of Geotown, a special kind of picture of a place called a *map*.

Compare and contrast the features on this map with those on the other two bands. The more that the children can develop their own understanding and definition of a map, the more likely they are to remember it. Eventually you will want them to understand this: Maps are tools. People use them so that they can find where and which way places are. Maps can find which places are near and which are far, maps are views from above, they are drawn to scale, and they use symbols to show information. Children will be able to use this geographic tool to answer many questions about the Earth.

3. Help the children analyze the characteristics of a map on their own. The following facts about the Geotown map in the bottom band should be firmly established by this activity:

○ This is a picture of Geotown, the same place they see in the other two bands.

○ This is a view from above, similar to the view in the middle band.

○ Places in Geotown are shown on the map with symbols.

○ They can use the map to find out where a place is.

○ The map shows what direction places are in relation to one another.

○ The map shows the distance between places.

○ The map is drawn on a small scale; it is a small picture of a large place.

As the children establish each of these points with the help of your examples and questions, write the key words on the board.

4. To practice reading the map, play a Round Robin question game. Begin by asking a question about the map. For example, "What building is to the left of the bank?" Let the child who correctly answers the question, ask the next.

Across The Curriculum

Linking Literature And Geography

Share with the class some books that include simple maps such as *Winnie the Pooh* by A. A. Milne (Dutton), *Araminta's Paint Box* by Karen Ackerman (Atheneum), and *John Tabor's Ride* by Blair Lent (Knopf).

Mapping The Geotown Zoo

Materials Needed

1. Reproducibles 12 (p. 92), 13 (p. 93), and 14 (p. 94)

2. Scissors

3. Paste

4. Crayons

Note: Children can work in pairs to make the map of the Geotown Zoo.

What To Do

1. Distribute one copy of Reproducible 12 to each child. Encourage them to study and talk about the picture of the Geotown Zoo. Tell them that they can make a map of the zoo. Help them review what they remember about this special kind of picture, and ask them what they will need to make a map.

2. Hand out Reproducibles 13 and 14 and explain that they can use the symbols on Reproducible 14 to make their map on Reproducible 13. After children cut out the symbols, have them match them to those in

the picture of the zoo on Reproducible 12. Then have them arrange the pieces correctly to make a map. Remind children that this is not a free drawing; they are reproducing an actual place—the zoo—pictured on Reproducible 12. They must place the symbols in the same places as they appear in the picture of the zoo.

3. After the children have placed all the pieces correctly, they can paste them down and then color their maps.

4. Working in small groups, children can practice using their maps. One child can announce what he or she wants to see at the zoo. For example, "First, I want to see the monkeys and then I want to go to the polar bears." The other children can trace the best route on the map. Encourage children to use direction words, like *left* and *right*, and distance words, like *near* and *far*, as they describe their trips through the zoo. Ask them how the map would help them get around the zoo and what problems would they have without a map.

Across The Curriculum

Linking Literature And Geography

Making a map based on a story is a bit more difficult, but children can do it with storybooks like *The Third Story Cat* by Leslie Baker (Little, Brown). Using this book, help children list the cat's adventures and draw a picture map of its travels.

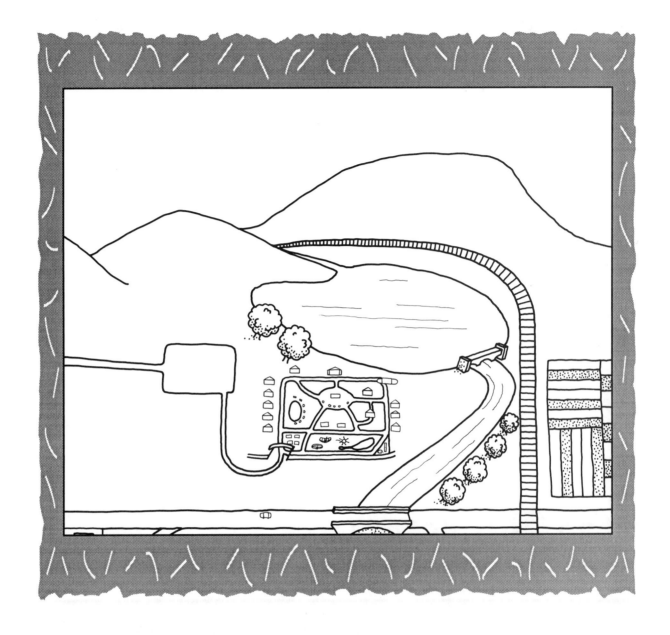

BEING A GEOGRAPHER

Before beginning the following activities, children should have used **Getting Started** or have been introduced to the basic components of a map in some other way. They should have an understanding that maps picture places from above, are drawn to scale, show distance and directions, and use symbols to show information. Once the students have a basic understanding of these concepts, they are ready to think in the more sophisticated geographic terms found in **Being a Geographer**.

In the first four sections of **Being a Geographer**, the children will be exposed to a wide variety of different kinds of maps and learn higher-level skills in direction, distance, and the use of symbols. The activities included in the last six sections will collectively help children look at the world around them as geographers. Individually, the activities will help children with the following:

○ to see how geographic features, like landforms and bodies of water, affect people;

○ to monitor climate and observe its effects;

○ to build models of their community to better see how it works;

○ to study the cause-and-effect relationships between location and economics;

○ to chart the changes in a place and its environment over time;

○ to plan for the future.

Creating A Geography Center

Just as access to books is essential to reading, exposure to maps is essential to geography. The creation of a *Geography Center* filled with maps and other resources is the greatest key to the world of geography that you can offer your children. The following are some ideas to help you create a Geography Center in your classroom:

Globes:

At least one globe is needed in a Geography Center. If possible several different types and sizes of globes can be displayed, including soft or inflatable globes children can hold and manipulate.

Maps:

It is important to collect a wide variety of maps. The children can be introduced to maps from stories, maps that are games, maps of small places, maps of large places, star maps, maps of ancient places, maps of future places, picture maps, road maps, maps of places nearby and far away, maps of the ocean floor, town maps that show sewer and electrical systems, bus and subway maps, maps of airports or parks or theaters, and on and on—the greater the variety, the better.

The best place to find suitable maps is to start close to home. Some sources for local maps are the library; historical societies; realty companies; the chamber of commerce; private, state, or federal parks or zoos; state or local tourist boards; local corporations or businesses; and local transportation systems.

Collect materials to compare and contrast with your region. Write to tourist boards requesting free maps and other materials in states that differ dramatically from your region.

Periodicals and travel agencies are a good source for international maps. *National Geographic, World* and *Traveler* magazines, travel sections in Sunday newspapers, and other travel magazines are wonderful resources that can be included in the Geography Center.

Create a boxed collection of state maps and another of maps of nations. This can become a wonderful class project involving parents. You can use Reproducible 41 (p. 121) to request home support for collecting maps.

The best maps for children are large-scale, that is, they are large pictures of small places, such as a town, a park, or a museum. Small-scale maps are small pictures of large places—a map of the world, for example. A large map of a neighborhood is much better for children than a small map of Alaska. There should be things on the map to give a sense of the place. Children love maps with pictorial symbols. Detailed maps are suitable for young children if the details excite their interest.

Some maps that are made for children are too simple. These maps have too little information on them and have a tendency to become too abstract and have little meaning to children. On the other hand, avoid maps that use symbols that are too abstract for the children to identify, —for example, most contour maps are too sophisticated for young children.

Atlases and Books About Geography:

Although most atlases are too complex for primary classrooms, exposure to any atlas is good and can pique children's curiosity. Look for variety. Some possibilities are:

- ○ *My First Atlas* by Kate Petty (Warner)
- ○ *Reader's Digest Children's World Atlas* (Random House)
- ○ *Scholastic Student Desk Atlas* (Scholastic)
- ○ *Children's Atlas of World Wildlife* (Rand McNally)
- ○ *The Children's Space Atlas* by Robin Kerrod (Millbrook)
- ○ *National Geographic Picture Atlas of Our Fifty States* (National Geographic)

Books about geography include:

- ○ *Geography from A to Z* and *Maps and Globes* by Jack Knowlton (Harper Collins)
- ○ *All Around the World* by Judy Donnelly (Grosset and Dunlap)
- ○ *What's in a Map?* by Sally Cartwright (Putnam)
- ○ *Around and About: Maps and Journeys* by Kate Petty and Jakki Wood (Barrons)

- ○ *Maps and Mapping* by Barbara Taylor (Kingfisher Books)

You may also want to include in the Geography Center any of the books that are recommended throughout this book in the **Linking Literature and Geography** feature.

Puzzles:

Available commercial puzzles include simple maps of the United States and the world. You may also want to mount maps on cardboard and cut them into puzzles.

Pictures:

Collect as many back issues as you can of magazines such as *National Geographic*, *World*, and other travel magazines. Families are often a wonderful source of old magazines. You can use Reproducible 41 (p. 121) to ask for them. Leave out some of these for children to leaf through and cut out pictures on their own. In addition, you may want to create picture collections based on the following categories:

- ○ Our Region: Include pictures of both local public and private buildings, landmarks, landforms, and any places that might appear on a local map.
- ○ Landforms: Include pictures of mountains, hills, plains, valleys, canyons, coastlines, rivers, lakes, streams, oceans, and so on.
- ○ Cold, Hot, and In-Between Places: Include pictures of polar and mountain-top regions, temperate regions in different seasons, and tropical places.
- ○ Land Use: Include pictures of farming, ranching, forestry, mining, industry, fishing, recreation, and any other use of land
- ○ Communities: Include pictures of different kinds of communities—rural, suburban, small towns, and large cities.

These picture collections can be added to by the children throughout the year. If you wish, you and the children can mount the pictures on lightweight cardboard or on chart paper to preserve them and make them easier to use. You might also allow all children to select a laminated picture or map to keep at their desks or tables.

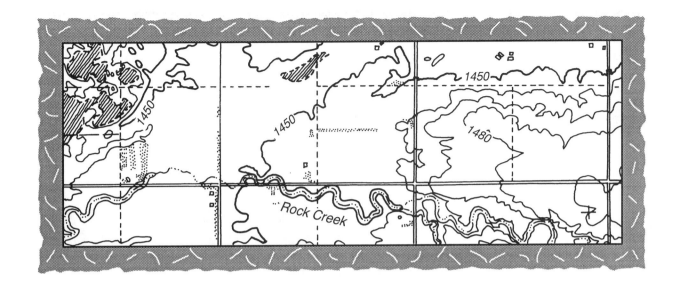

MAPS, MAPS, MAPS
Using Your Geography Center

One of a geographer's most important tools, maps are geographic pictures of places. For many children, however, maps reside only in their social studies textbooks or on the walls of their classrooms, receiving very little attention or interest. By exposing children to a wide variety of maps and giving them reasons and opportunities to use them, you will open their eyes to a wider world—literally and figuratively. The following activities will help children review what they have learned about maps and introduce them to the treasures of your Geography Center.

Being A Map Detective

Since maps come in all sizes, shapes, and types, children need a clear understanding of their essential characteristics in order to distinguish a map from another kind of picture of a place. This activity will help them review these characteristics in the process of identifying and categorizing different kinds of views of a place.

Materials Needed

1. Poster (Side 1)

2. Reproducibles 15 (p. 95) and 16 (p. 96)

3. Scissors

4. Crayons

Before Starting

Prepare by displaying the Poster (Side 1) and cutting, mounting—and coloring, if you wish—

copies of Reproducibles 15 and 16 for demonstration.

What To Do

1. Begin a discussion with the children about what a map is and when and how we use maps. You may want to begin a "KWL" chart with the class (that is, a chart with columns having the following titles:" What We Know about Maps," "What We Want to Know about Maps," and—to be filled in later—"What We Learned about Maps").

2. Let the children themselves describe the common characteristics of maps, guiding them with questions such as: "What do maps show?" and "What can you find out by using a map?" Among other characteristics that are discussed, the children should know that maps are views from above, use symbols, are small-scale drawings of larger places, and enable you to determine location, direction, and distance. Then ask the children if they see any maps in the room. When someone has identified the map on Poster (Side 1) ask them to tell you how they know that the picture in the third band (Band C) is a map. Through guided discussion help the children recognize the characteristics listed above. Invite them to compare the three bands, discussing their likenesses and differences.

3. Now invite the children to be "map detectives". Show them the aerial view and the map of Old Town Square from Reproducibles 15 and 16. Let children point out similarities and differences between the map and the picture.

4. Distribute copies of Reproducible 15 and 16 to the children. Have them cut out all of the pictures on the two reproducibles. Then ask them to match the aerial view and the map of each of the four places in Geotown.

5. Invite the children to color their picture and map cards. However, before they begin, ask them to think about the way that color is used on the map of Geotown. Children should see that in "real life," houses, for example, may be many different colors, but on the map the symbol for a house is the same color throughout.

Introducing Your Geography Center

Introducing children to the Geography Center will serve several purposes at this point: to excite and intrigue the children's curiosity about the wide variety of maps, to help them see maps as real-life tools rather than merely textbook or classroom exercises, and to stimulate their desire to learn more about how to read complex maps.

Materials Needed

1. Poster (Side 2)

2. Reproducible 41 (p. 00)

3. Maps and globes

4. Local maps

5. Photographs or pictures of local places

6. Yarn or colored string

7. Push pins

Before Starting

Display one or more local maps on a wall or bulletin board near the Geography Center.

What To Do

1. Introduce children to the Geography Center and allow them to browse through the maps

and globes you have collected. Tell them something about where you obtained the various maps and encourage any and all questions about them, especially questions about who uses the maps and how. Pick up a map you might use yourself—a road map or map of a local area—and tell the children when and how you actually use this map. Discuss the other maps in the same way, asking the children for personal experiences when they have seen someone using a map.

2. To give children more insights into the differences in the maps and their uses, show them a map of a single nation. Then help the children find that nation on the globe. Pose questions that can be answered by looking at the globe and then the map. Let the children identify ways in which the globe and the map differ. Then show them a map of a larger area that includes the same nation—for example, show a map of the United States and then a map of North America—and talk about what the children can find out from each map.

The point of all of this is not for children to actually read these maps, which may be too complicated for them at this point. Rather, it is for them to begin to sense the many different ways that maps and globes can show the same place, as well as the different kinds of information that they can get from them.

3. You can also tap the children's innate curiosity about how to read these maps. A good place to start is with a fairly simple local map that includes devices the children are not yet familiar with, such as a compass rose and a distance scale. Have children study the local map or maps that you have displayed and ask them if there is anything on the maps that they have never seen before. Have them speculate on the uses of these devices and tell them that they will be learning how to use them over the next few weeks. Finally, display Poster (Side 2) and let children compare the map on this side with the simpler map on Side 1, Band C.

4. If you have gathered some photographs or pictures of local places that are shown on your local map, you can help children connect these real places with the symbols on the local map. Help children identify the places in the pictures and locate them on the map. You might want to display the pictures around the map, connecting pictures and locations with colored string or yarn and push pins.

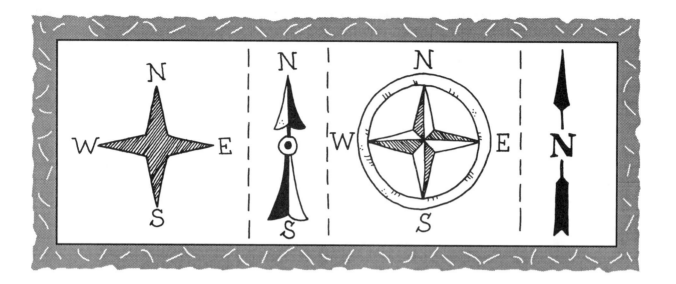

ALL AROUND THE GLOBE
Using Cardinal Directions

If children have a strong grounding in direction from their work in the **Getting Started** part of this book, they should have little trouble translating front, back, right, and left into the cardinal directions of north, south, east, and west. Since all children love to feel competent and grown-up, they will enjoy the easy acquisition of cardinal directions.

Understanding Why We Need Cardinal Directions

As we all know, children learn best when they understand why they are learning. Begin with a game that demonstrates the need for a fixed reference point in giving directions. Along with the fun and the confusion, children should recognize the need to learn something new.

What To Do

1. Have the children stand and face randomly in many different directions. Tell them that the object of the game is to end up with the whole class facing in the same direction. The rules are as follows: The only commands that can be used are to tell someone to turn right or left. No one can be called by name. The commands may be: "Everyone with yellow boots, turn right," or "The persons with glasses turn left," and so on.

2. Start the game by giving the first few commands, yourself. Then allow the children to take turns giving commands. The situation will, and should, become highly confused.

3. Discuss with the children better ways of instructing them to face in one direction. They should arrive at the concept of a fixed point of reference even if they are not able to articulate it. Ask if anyone can think of one

direction that, if broadcast all around the Earth, would make everyone face toward the same place. If no one says *north*, *south*, *east*, or *west*, write the words on the board.

Learning The Cardinal Directions

When learning cardinal directions, the North Pole is most often used as a point of reference. However, it can be difficult for young children to visualize the North Pole's location, even for those who have seen the Earth from space on television. This activity should help them understand this.abstract concept.

Materials Needed

1. Reproducible 6 (p. 86 figures only)

2. Globes

3. Small toy figure or doll

Before Starting

Place one globe at each worktable or cluster of desks so that a small group of children can work together. Have the children cut out the figures from Reproducible 6.

Note: Try to do the next two activities on the same or consecutive days.

What To Do

1. Ask the children to point north. Some may know the direction; others may point up or simply not know. Tell the class that north is always in the same direction, no matter where

you are on the Earth. Ask if anyone knows how that is possible.

2. Explain that north is the direction going toward the North Pole. Ask if anyone knows where the North Pole is. Help children locate it at the top of each globe. (The trick here may be extricating yourself from any discussions of the North Pole as the place where Santa Claus lives!)

3. Ask a child to put his or her finger on the North Pole on the globe and then place the toy or paper figure on the United States on the same globe. As the child moves the figure toward the North Pole, ask in which direction he or she is moving. Repeat this, placing the figure on various parts of the globe, including southern Africa and South America. Have the other children do the same thing on their globes, "walking" their figures toward the North Pole.

4. Repeat the same procedure to teach south and the South Pole.

5. Ask the children if anyone can name two other directions. If children do not name east and west, tell them that there are two other main directions and name them. Explain that when you face north, east is on your right and west is on your left. The activities that follow will reinforce understanding of this east/right, west/left connection.

Across The Curriculum

Linking Literature and Geography

Two books with which children could practice using directions on the globe are *Jeremy's Tail* by Duncan Ball (Orchard Books) and *Henny's World Tour* by Robert Quackenbush (Doubleday). Both stories are excellent for children to use to trace the traveler's routes on the globe, describing the directions as they go.

Using The Sun To Find North

North ←

Materials Needed

1. Chalk

2. 2 small stickers for the thumbs of each child

Before Starting

Place a small sticker marked "E" or "East" on each child's right thumb and another marked "W" or "West" on the left thumb.

Note: This activity must be done outdoors around noon on a sunny day. It will work best if you do it on a playground or other surface that you can mark with chalk.

What To Do

1. In this activity the children will learn how to find north using the sun. Point out to the class that they have learned how to find north on a model of the Earth; now they are going to learn a way to find north on the real Earth. Tell them that they are going to take a trip outdoors to find north.

2. Invite children to find a direction to face so that their shadows are straight in front of them. Explain that this is a way of being sure that they are facing north. When their shadows are straight in front of them at midday, the top of them—that is, the shadows of their heads—are pointing north. Remind the children that when they point north, they are pointing to the North Pole. To reinforce the understanding of this direction and to make a connection with the compass rose (that you are going to draw later), draw arrows pointing north at the tips of the children's shadows.

3. Now ask children where south is and lead them to the conclusion that south is in back of them—the opposite of north.

4. Ask the children to identify the other two main directions (east and west). As they face north, ask them to extend their arms straight out from their sides and wiggle their thumbs that point east and then the thumbs that point west. Vary the hand actions to snapping fingers, moving the hands up and down, and so on, in a Simon Says game giving the children plenty of practice in indicating east and west.

5. Invite all the children to face south. Ask them if their right hands still point east. When they discover that the right/east and left/west relationships are just the opposite when they are facing south, suggest they cross their arms in front of them so that the markers are pointing in the correct directions to indicate east and west. Help children see that no matter what direction they face, the cardinal directions remain in the same position.

6. Use chalk to draw a large compass rose on the ground labeled with "north," "south," "east" and "west." If you do not wish to mark your schoolyard, make a compass rose on a large piece of poster board. Explain that a drawing like this that shows the directions is called a "compass rose."

7. Have the children identify visible landmarks like a building, a stop sign, or a fire hydrant as being north, south, east, or west of where they are standing. The compass rose can help them. Encourage them to walk toward various spots on the playground and tell in which direction they are going.

4. Have the children identify objects within the classroom as being north, south, east, or west of them using their compass roses.

5. Culminate the activity by having them create labels to show south, east, and west in the classroom. Display these labels, in their appropriate places, encouraging the children to refer to them often for the rest of the year.

Creating And Orienting A Compass Rose

Materials Needed

1. Reproducible 17 (p. 97)

2. Crayons or colored markers

Before Starting

Use a compass to identify true north in the classroom and label it on the wall with the word "north."

What To Do

1. Distribute copies of Reproducible 17 and help the children identify the compass roses and north arrows at the bottom of the page. Tell them that they are going to create and use their own compass roses now.

2. Have children find north on the drawing of the Earth on Reproducible 17, then create their designs using the drawing of the Earth as the center of their compass roses.

3. To correctly orient their compass roses, have the students turn their art work until their north arrows point to the north sign in the room. Allowing flexible seating will make this activity easier to do.

Practicing Cardinal Directions

Reinforce the children's understanding of cardinal directions by using the game of Simon Says and the poster map.

Materials Needed

1. Poster (Side 2)

2. Compasses

What To Do

1. Play a game of Simon Says using north, south, east, and west for the commands. Remind children to use the labels on the classroom walls as they turn. Help them see that the cardinal directions are real, not relative directions; that is, they are always in the same direction from any given point. Remind the class of the problems they encountered in their earlier game when they could only use the directions to turn left or right.

2. Ask the children to look at the Poster (Side 2) of Geotown. Have someone point out the compass rose on the map and identify the four directions.

3. Have a volunteer place his or her fingers in a "walking" position on the map and have another play Simon to direct the walker using

commands such as, "Simon says walk north." and "Simon says turn west at the next street."

4. Divide the children into groups of 4 or 5. Let one group hide a "treasure" in the classroom and direct another group of children to find it by following clues based on the cardinal directions. When the group finds the treasure, they can hide it again and provide the clues for finding it.

5. You may want to introduce a real compass to the children and show them how to use it. If possible, provide a compass for each group or each child to use at the same time. Allow the children to walk freely around the room holding the compasses. They will observe that the needle always points to the north sign on the classroom wall.

Using The Cardinal Directions

Materials Needed

1. Reproducibles 18 (p. 98) and 19 (p. 99)

2. Scissors

3. Crayons

Before Starting

Have the children work together to cut out the picture elements from Reproducible 19 (top left corner.) Coloring in each picture may make it easier for children to keep track of and identify the picture elements as they play.

What To Do

1. As you read the story below, allow time for the children to place the manipulatives in the correct places on their maps on Reproducible 18.

Willy and the Four Directions

Willy has four special friends named "West," "South," "East," and "North." As a group they are called "The Four Directions." These friends help Willy find his way, wherever he wants to go.

Today is the Geotown County Fair and Willy asks to go. "All right," says Willy's mom, "but you must stay with your friends, the Four Directions, for they will show you the way." So off they go to the fairground—Willy and his friends, West, South, East, and North.

Find the entrance to the fair. This is where the story begins. Place your picture of a ticket booth at the entrance.

The first thing Willy wants to see is which rabbits won a prize this year. North leads the way saying, "North we'll go and then you'll know." And so, north they go. They stop at the first booth. *Walk north from the entrance and stop at the first booth. Put a prize winning bunny there.*

Then, on the loudspeaker, Willy hears, "Attention please, it's geese feeding time in the east tent."

"Follow me," says East, "to the geese feast." And so they turn their backs on the rabbits and walk east across the fairgrounds. *Now you go east and put a feasting goose in the booth at the end of the road.*

Willy now wants to see the little pigs race. Their race track is north of where he is, but Willy isn't sure which way that is. North says, "Follow me and you will see." And so off to the north they go, all the way to the end of the road. *Now you go north and place a racing pig at the end of the road.*

The racing pigs were loads of fun and Willy's favorite won. Now Willy wants to see which sheep weighs the most this year. West says, "I'll take you west to find which sheep's the best." And so west they go, all the way to the end of the road. *Now you go west and put the big sheep at the end of the road.*

The day was fun, but it's just about done. Willy is ready to start for home. But which way will bring Willy back to where he had begun? [*Pause so the children can discover the way to go.*] So South says, "Follow me south and you'll get back to where we started from. And so south they go to where they had begun.

2. Give children a chance to compare their maps and the placement of the manipulatives, and to color in the rest of the fair.

3. You might also have the class imagine a storm with thunder and lightning. The frightened animals break out of their enclosures. Pigs, rabbits, horses, sheep, chickens, and cows all run around and around the fairgrounds. Have the children change the positions of the manipulatives to show where the animals go. They may add new manipulatives from Reproducible 19 or draw some of their own. Encourage the children to make up stories based on the new arrangements. These situations can be the basis for creative drama experiences.

Across The Curriculum

Linking Literature And Geography

Katy and the Big Snow by Virginia Lee Burton (Houghton, Mifflin) is a perfect book to read to the children at this point. The book even includes a compass rose on page 7 that children can use to plot the directions which Katy, the snow shovel, takes as she plows out the town of Geoppolis. Point out to the children that north is not at the top of this map, just as it may not be in the front of their classroom. Alert viewers will also spot the intermediate directions—northeast, southeast, northwest, southwest—labeled with initials on this compass rose. Tell them that these are the in-between directions. They may then arrive at the obvious names for the

directions between north and east, south and west, and so on.

A LONG WAY
Using Distance Scales

Calculating distance is one of the most common reasons why we adults use maps, but this can be a difficult skill for young children to acquire. Translating the difference between full-scale, or real, distance and the map measurement is often confusing. The more practice children have, the better.

Translating Actual Distance To A Map

Because it is often confusing for children to relate an unseen large distance to the specific small distance on a map, they need a chance to measure both and then compare the real measurements of the two.

Materials Needed

1. Local map
2. Large ball of string or twine
3. Clipboard
4. Pencil
5. Colored pencils
6. Ruler
7. Paper
8. Rock or weight

Before Starting

1. Plan a short walk near the school, of a distance that you can measure with your ball of string—say, 500 feet. (Unrolling a long length of string may be a bit tricky, so you'll need to determine a distance that will be practical!) The walk should be in a straight

line, if possible. You can also do this activity in the school hallway or any large area.

2. Prepare the ball of string by marking it off in 10-foot lengths.

What To Do

1. Review with the children the basic principles of scale, (See Getting Started, pages 20-23) letting them describe small things that stand for larger things, like model cars or dolls. Then point to the map of their community and ask children why the map is smaller than the real community. The children will undoubtedly think that is a silly question—they are correct—but encourage them to imagine the difficulties of using an enormous map. Ask them how they think that people go about drawing small maps. How do they know what to put where and what distances to use. Explain that they are going to make a map themselves to see how it is done.

2. With a clipboard, paper, and pencil in your hand, bring the children to the starting point of the walk. Explain that when they return to the classroom, they will draw a map of the walk starting at this point. So that the children can see how far they have walked, they are going to measure with a string. Have children tie or weight one end of the string, and ask volunteers to unroll the ball of string as they walk. Special "string watchers" can call out the distance every 10 feet when they see the mark on the string, and others can tally each distance of 10 feet.

3. As they proceed, have the children identify things to put on the map—houses, stores, parks, and so on. List their suggestions as you walk.

4. When the full length of string is used, help the children to see how far they have walked by counting the lengths of 10 that the string watchers have tallied. Rewind the string and bring it back to the classroom.

5. Upon returning to the classroom, discuss with the children how big to make the map. Ask them to unroll the length of string showing the length of their walk. Let them talk about why they cannot make their map that large.

6. Your discussion with the children of ways to determine the size of the map will be shaped by their abilities to understand mathematical relationships. There are several ways to go about translating actual distance into map measurement. Children can use graph paper, deciding what length each square should represent. They can count off the correct number of squares to show the route.

Or, you could assign an actual ratio in inches and feet, like, "One inch stands for 50 feet." Then working together, the children can assign actual distance for each number of inches. "If 1 inch stands for 50 feet, 2 inches will stand for 50 more feet, or 100 feet altogether."

7. You may want to have the whole class work on one map or have the children work in small groups on several maps. Have the children use a ruler to draw a line of the determined length across a sheet of paper. Ask the children if this is a map yet. Children should recognize that this is not yet a picture of a place; it needs more information on it.

8. Ask children what they'd like to show on the map and remind them of the list of places you made on the walk. Read the list aloud and write it on the board. Discuss why things that move are not usually included on maps.

Talk with the children about how they want to show the places. Since the purpose of this activity is understanding the relationship between the real distance and the map measurements, children may not think about symbols. The easiest map for them to make will be a picture map such as those on the poster. Have the students use colored pencils to add pictures to the route they have drawn. They can include any or all of the information on the list or add other information that they recall. Encourage them to remember where things were on the walk and to locate them as correctly as possible on their maps.

9. When their maps are complete, write the distance/measurement ratio like "One inch stands for 50 feet," or "One block stands for 50 feet," on the board and have the children copy it onto their maps.

Measuring Distance In Geotown

In this activity children learn to use a simple distance scale on a map.

Materials Needed

1. Poster (Side 2)
2. Yarn
3. Scissors

What To Do

1. Ask the children if they can find anything on the Geotown map that tells them what distance the map shows. When they spot the distance scale, guide them in understanding what it shows.

2. Have a volunteer cut a piece of yarn the length of the distance scale. The children will use the yarn to measure distances on the map. For example, have a child place one end of the yarn at the bank on Main Street and move the other end from place to place. Ask children where they would be if they walked x feet from the bank. Children can relate map distance and actual distance using different starting points. Repeat this with other children, by describing a situation like, "The post office and the police station are 2 inches apart on the map. That means they are really 100 feet apart."

3. Do the same thing using a string that is double the length of the distance scale. Then depending on your children's math skills have them measure distances one-half the scale.

4. If you wish, measure yarn lengths to match the distance scale on your local map and let the children measure the distances from school to home. This activity can be repeated on any map from one place to another. Large-scale maps of familiar places work best for this kind of practice.

Across The Curriculum

Linking Math And Geography

Use the data collected when the children measured the distance from school to home as the basis for chart and graph activities. Set up categories of distances—for example," More Than 1 Mile from School" and "Less Than 1 Mile from School"—and have the children write their names in the correct categories on the chart. Children can draw pictures of themselves on a pictograph or create bar graphs using the same data. You can do the same with other categorizations, such as children who live north of the school, south of the school, and so on.

Plotting Distance On A Map

Materials Needed

1. Reproducible 20 (p. 100)
2. Yarn
3. Colored pencils or crayons

Before Starting

Cut lengths of yarn for each child or small group that match the length of the distance scale on Reproducible 20.

What To Do

1. Have children work in pairs to measure distances on the reproducible in response to the following story problem:

   Tama and Jake have a set of walkie-talkies that work within 100 feet. If Tama is at the pet store, can Jake hear her from the bank?

   Ask the children to mark a "T" at the pet store on their map. Then mark a "J" at three different places where Jake can hear Tama.

2. Ask the children to "go shopping" in Geotown. Each pair of children should decide what they will do if they have an hour to spend on Main Street on Saturday morning. Have them mark their stops and use the yarn to find the approximate distance they will walk on their trip.

3. Again, you could repeat this activity with local maps, posing problems that name familiar landmarks. This will help the students to better associate real places with the map symbols. If you have any children who are new in the neighborhood, photographs of key locations will be helpful in this activity.

Orienteering On Main Street In Geotown

The sport of *orienteering* is a most exciting way to learn map reading. It demands an understanding of scale and directions that builds not only skills, but self esteem as well. This in-class version of orienteering will allow children to practice their skills with a goal.

Materials Needed

1. Reproducibles 19 (p. 99), and 21 (p. 101)
2. Scissors
3. Pencils

Before Starting

Use Reproducible 42 (p. 122) to make a blue ribbon for each child in the class.

What To Do

1. Ask the children to cut out the distance scale and score card from Reproducible 19. Ask if anyone has ever gone on a treasure or scavenger hunt and have them explain what they did. Explain that now they are going to hunt for places in a special kind of treasure hunt called orienteering.

2. Allow plenty of time for them to use their scales, recall the cardinal directions, and move their markers on Reproducible 21. Then, read the following instructions to the children:

   ○ Put your marker on the starting square facing west. In this game you do not need to follow the paths. Your marker can go in a straight line crossing the grass and paths.

   ○ What do you see in front of you? Find that picture on your score card and put the number 1 next to it.

   ○ Turn north and go 70 feet. What is there? Find that picture on your score card and put the number 2 next to it.

❍ Turn east and go 20 feet. What are you in front of now? Find it on your score card and put the number 3 next to it.

❍ Go another 60 feet east. What are you in front of now? Find it on your score card and put a number 4 next to it.

❍ Turn south and go 90 feet. Then turn east and what do you see? Find it on your card and put the number 5 next to it.

❍ Turn west and go 50 feet. What are you in front of now? Put a number 6 next to its picture on the score card.

3. When the children's score cards have been completed, have them check their own cards. *Answers: 1–statue, 2–restaurant, 3–pet store, 4–children's park, 5–flag pole, 6–fountain.* Hand out blue ribbons as Orienteering Prizes to all who participated in the game.

4. Students can write individually or as a class to find out more about orienteering.

United States Orienteering Federation

P.O. Box 1444

Forest Park, GA 30051

Ask for information about the Little Troll program, which is orienteering designed for young children.

Finding Your Global Address

Finding their own community on a series of maps can give children a beginning sense of their place in the larger world. At the same time, it will help them see that map scales vary from smaller areas to scales encompassing thousands of miles.

Materials Needed

1. Set of maps from the Geography Center

(showing increasingly larger areas—your community, your state, the United States, North America, the Western Hemisphere, the world)

2. Set of nesting measuring cups or boxes

Before Starting

Put the maps in order, from smallest to largest area covered.

What To Do

1. Display the series of maps in the order of the area covered and ask children how they think they differ from each other. Ask for someone to point to the map of the smallest place and then to that of the largest place.

2. Beginning with the map of their community, help the children locate the approximate position of their school. Then help them find the name of their community on the state map. The next step is to find the state on the map of the United States. Then help the children find the United States on the continent, hemisphere, and world maps. If children in your class have come from other countries, they can find those countries on the larger maps as well. Ask these children to tell how they traveled to the United States.

3. Display a set of nesting cups or boxes unnested. Allow the children to arrange the set so that one container fits into the other until all are inside the largest container. Encourage them to discuss how the set of cups and boxes are like the set of maps.

4. Discuss the value of different kinds of maps. Ask the children which map would be most useful for locating their homes, and which would be best for planning a trip from their town to Washington, D.C.

5. Ask the children to find the distance scale on each map and tell you what it says. List these on the board from smallest area map to largest. Although they cannot at this point make any complicated calculations using these scales, children can begin to see the differences in the distances shown on each map.

6. Finally, ask the children to label the set of cups; for example, label the smallest as your town and the largest as the continent (if you have four cups). Ask children to imagine themselves standing in the smallest cup. Then show them how to write their global address (i.e., name, street address, town, state, country, continent, hemisphere, and planet).

Across The Curriculum

Linking Literature And Geography

My *Place in Space* by Robin and Sally Hirst (Orchard Books) is an engaging book in which a young boy gives his global address—actually, his universal address—to the nth degree. Although the information on astronomy may seem too advanced for young children, they will be fascinated by the beautiful paintings of the solar system and amused by the book's tone and story.

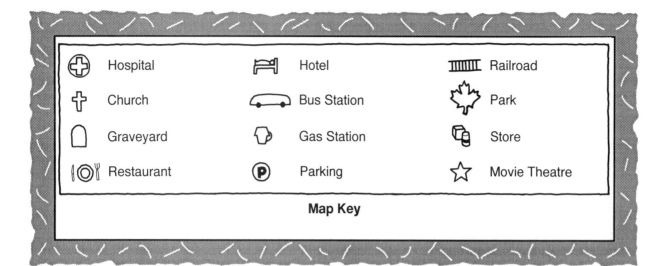

⊕	Hospital	⊨	Hotel	▥	Railroad
✝	Church	☞	Bus Station	🍁	Park
⌂	Graveyard	⬮	Gas Station	▦	Store
🍽	Restaurant	Ⓟ	Parking	☆	Movie Theatre

Map Key

WHAT'S WHAT
Using Symbols

People are symbol-using beings. From cave people to rocket scientists, people have used symbols to describe the heavens and the world around them. With symbols to describe every natural or cultural phenomena known, some of these signs, like alphabets and traffic lights, have become standardized. Map symbols, however, are not standardized. There is no dictionary of map symbols. Each map or set of maps has its own system. These activities will guide children through the ways and means of understanding, using, and creating map symbols as they move from their first picture maps to more abstract and sophisticated symbol systems.

Understanding Symbols On The Map Of Geotown

The set of pictures and maps on the two sides of the poster provides children with a useful progression from pictures to pictorial symbols to abstract symbols of the same places.

Materials Needed

Poster (Sides 1 and 2)

What To Do

1. Display the Poster (Side 1) and have children review the three different views of Geotown. Invite the children to compare and contrast the different portrayals of the same places and buildings, going back and forth from one to the other.

2. Display the Poster (Side 2) Help each child find his or her special place or building on the map on the bottom half of the poster and discuss how it differs from the Side 1

depictions. Talk about why simple symbols are useful if many different kinds of places and buildings are being shown. In the process, guide children toward a definition of a symbol as a picture or color that stands for a thing or idea.

3. Have children find the map key on Side 2. Help them connect the meaning of the word *key* as something that unlocks a door, with this use of key as unlocking the door to understanding a map. Have volunteers point to a symbol in the key and then find examples of the same thing on the map.

Reinforcing An Understanding Of Symbols

Matching pictures and symbols in a variety of games helps reinforce children's understanding of abstract symbols. Here are several games that children will love to play.

Materials Needed

1. Poster (Side 2)

2. Reproducible 22 (p. 102)

3. Scissors

Before Starting

Have children cut out the cards from their copies of Reproducible 22 and divide them into groups of symbols and pictures.

What To Do

1. Play Match It Up with the class. Point on the map to one of the symbols in the map key. As you point, name the landmark. Ask the children to find the symbol on the map and in their set of cards. They can hold their cards so

that no one can see them until the whole class reveals its cards. Ask a child who chose the correct card to explain how he or she did it. Then give everyone a chance to find the correct cards and check them against the map. Follow the same procedure with the other landmarks. Learning partners can play this game with each another, if time allows.

2. Children can play Memory or Concentration in groups of two or three. First, lay all the cards face down in an array. One player turns over one card and leaves it face up. The player then turns over one more card. If the two cards are a pair (i.e., if they are the picture and symbol for the same place), the player removes the two cards from the table and takes another turn. If the two are not a pair, the player turns both cards back face down and the next player takes a turn. The player who collects the most cards wins.

3. Children can play a version of Go Fish in groups of two or three. Each player (we'll call them Molly and Willy) is dealt one card. The remaining cards are placed face down in a stack. Molly goes first. She chooses one card from the stack and asks Willy if he has its mate to make a picture/symbol pair. If Willy has the card, he must give it to Molly, who now has a pair and takes another turn. If not, Willy says, "Go Fish," and Molly draws a card from the stack. Now it is Willy's turn to "fish" for a card. When any player is out of cards, he or she is allowed to draw from the pile and go again. When all of the cards have been drawn, the player with the most pairs is the winner.

Using Symbols To Map Geotown

The act of transforming a picture map into a symbolic map gives children a stronger understanding of what the symbols stand for. This procedure is a powerful reinforcement of the direct correlation between a symbol and a place.

Materials Needed

1. Reproducibles 23 (p.103) and 24 (p. 104)

2. Scissors

3. Crayons or colored pencils

4. Paste

What To Do

1. Distribute a copy of Reproducible 23 to each child or to each pair of children. Ask them to describe what they see in the picture. Have them name places that are shown.

2. Distribute copies of Reproducible 24. Tell the children that they are can use these symbols to make a new map of Geotown. Direct their attention to the larger symbols on the top half of the sheet and ask them to cut them out and match them to the correct places in the map.

3. To help the children understand the importance of matching symbol to picture, ask them who might use this map (someone who wants to find places in Geotown). The symbols have to be in the correct places for the user to find his or her way around Geotown.

4. When the symbols are pasted down, ask the children how someone will know what each symbol means. After a child suggests that the map needs a key, have children use the bottom half of Reproducible 24 to make a key for the map.

5. Children can explore different symbol systems by comparing maps and their keys in the Geography Center. Set up a "treasure hunt" based on the maps that you have in the center. For example, ask children to find three different ways that maps show roads or airports. Ask them to find a map that has symbols for animals. Ask them to show you two different ways that maps show water. All of this will be possible, even for primary children, if the maps in the center are simple enough.

Across The Curriculum

Linking Art And Geography

When children have explored the many different ways in which map makers draw symbols, let them create their own symbol systems. Encourage the children to make up a list of places and buildings one might see on a map. Then have children draw pairs of pictures and symbols. If they draw these on small pieces of paper or index cards, other children can try to match the pairs correctly.

Making A Map Of A Desk

By making their own maps of a very small place—their desks—children will combine several map skills that they have learned. You may wish to have children map their individual desks, or you may prefer to set up one or two tables in the classroom for all children to map.

Materials Needed

1. Paper

2. Colored pencils

3. Miscellaneous objects to be placed on each desk

What To Do

1. Tell children that they are going to have a chance to make maps of places that they

know very well—their desks. Even though no one would actually ever need a map of a desk, this activity will give them an idea of how people make maps.

2. Ask the children to arrange a few small objects on their desks in any way they wish. Discuss with them how they will show these objects on their maps. You may want to have them first draw pictures of their desktops. Then, they can create a symbol for each thing in the pictures. They can then draw maps of the desktops using symbols in place of pictures.

3. Children can use these maps to review some of the basic characteristics of maps; namely, that they are views from above, that they show location, that maps represent reality with symbols.

4. The children may enjoy the challenge of mapping their rooms at home.

LAND AND WATER
Learning About Physical Geography

Imagine a person who knows nothing about this nation—someone who has never heard of New York or Los Angeles, of the "Breadbasket" or the "Cotton Belt." Now imagine this person with a good landforms map. They can now point out the huge cities of the coastal plains, the industrial cities of the Great Lakes, the centers of trade on the Missouri/Mississippi river system, the farms of the Midwest, and the ranches of the western plains. They can even tell you where to ski or where to sunbathe. Though we usually take them for granted, geographical features—landforms and bodies of water—determine much of the world around us. These activities are meant to introduce children to physical geography and its effects upon their lives.

All of these will be much richer if you can collect a number of photographs that show geographical features. Travel magazines and postcard collections are good sources of pictures. You may also want to enlist families and friends to take photographs of local geographic features.

Identifying Geographical Features In Geotown

Use the geography of the children's own community—as well as the pictures of Geotown and its surroundings—to help children give names to the shapes of the land and kinds of bodies of water.

Materials Needed

1. Poster (Side 2)

2. Reproducible 25 (p. 105)

3. Photographs of geographic features

4. Clay or playdough

What To Do

1. Begin by asking the children to think about what the land looks like outside of the school. Is it flat or hilly? Is there any water nearby? Expand the imaging to the larger community and its surroundings. Are there any very high places nearby? Any big rivers? An ocean? Write on the board all the names of geographic features that children offer.

2. At this point, let children look through the collection of pictures and find some that look like the land and water in their area. Each child or pair of children may choose one picture to talk about.

3. Explain to the children that the different shapes of the land are called *landforms*. Rivers, lakes, and oceans are called *bodies of water*. Invite them to tell how they would describe each of these landforms and bodies of water to someone who had never seen it before. Write the definitions on the board or on a piece of chart paper and ask the children to add to them or revise them as they work.

4. Call attention to Geotown's geographical setting at the top of Poster (Side 2) and distribute copies of Reproducible 25. Tell the class that Geotown is in quite an amazing place, surrounded by many different kinds of landforms. Have children find on the poster or reproducible all of the landforms that they have already identified. You may want to have them circle them on the reproducible.

5. Have the children color in all of the water on the reproducible, tracing the water back through the river to the lake.

6. Have children go back to the picture collection and match photographs to different places on the reproducible or poster.

7. Use a map of their local area for children to locate and name landforms and bodies of water nearby. Encourage the children to classify the local geographic features in such ways as, "There are three lakes and one river in our area." If there is surface water in the area—a stream, river, or stream-fed lake—children can have a wonderful time finding out where the water comes from and where it goes. As the water's course is discovered by the children, encourage them to use the correct geographical terms to describe what happens. For example, "The water starts in the mountains and flows through a valley to the plains." Some of the children may want to create a three-dimensional model of the area using clay or playdough.

Across The Curriculum

Linking Language And Geography

Children can make a *GeoDictionary* with their definitions of geographic features. They can write one definition on each page and draw an illustration to accompany it. Have them arrange the pages in alphabetical order in a looseleaf notebook. This way, they can insert new pages in the appropriate spots as they learn new terms. *Geography from A to Z* by Jack Knowlton (HarperCollins) is a useful resource to help children verify their definitions.

Playing A Game Of Geo-Bingo To Identify Landforms

Materials Needed

1. Reproducibles 26 (p. 106) and 27 (p. 107)

2. Scissors

3. Paste or tape

4. Chart paper

Before Starting

1. Write the following words across the board: *river, island, coastline, hill, valley, lake, mountain, plain* .

   Have the children write one of these words in each box of their GeoBingo card from Reproducible 26. It is important that they mix up the order of the words, using each one at least once.

2. Have children cut out the landform pictures from Reproducible 27 and sort them into piles of the same image. (It may be helpful for children to color the water blue on each card.)

What To Do

1. To begin the game of GeoBingo, a caller picks a landform from the landform pictures and identifies it by name only. It is important that no one else sees the picture selected.

2. The players match the correct pictures to words on their cards. Children may find it easier to paste or tape the pictures to the card. The first player to have four pictures in a row—diagonally, horizontally, or vertically—calls out "GeoBingo" and wins the game.

3. Children may select from the remaining landform pictures the features found near their community. Ask which, if any, features are missing, and have children create their pictures of these, using the backs of the unused cutouts.

Across The Curriculum

Linking Math And Geography

The class can make bar graphs using the cutouts and a piece of chart paper. Write the eight names of landforms listed above, across the bottom of a piece of chart paper. Then ask children to select the place they would most like to live in or near. Children can color the cards of their choice, write their names on them, and paste them in columns over the appropriate word. Remind the children to create a title for the bar graph. You may also want to ask children to think and write about why they picked the places they did.

Connecting Landforms And Human Activities

Children know that they can't water ski or fish where there is no water, but they may not have thought much beyond this about the relationships between geography and human action. As with so many things, they know a lot already but may not have made the possible connections. The story in this activity can help them do that.

Materials Needed

1. Reproducibles 25 (p. 105)

2. Colored pencils

What To Do

1. Distribute a copy of Reproducible 25 to each child. Tell the children that within the story you are going to give some directions and that you will pause while they mark their maps.

Nora's Trip

Nora is a very adventurous dog. One day, when she was bored, she decided to take a trip. She started in Geotown, where she lives. *Find*

Geotown in the picture and mark a 1 there.[*Help children use geographical landmarks as clues to locate Geotown: near the mountains, on the river, by the lake.*] Nora thought she'd better start out with an easy walk, on nice flat ground. So she went to visit David and Katie in Cityville. Draw a line to show how Help children use geographical landmarks as clues to locate geotown: near the mountains, on the river, by the lake. Nora walked to Cityville. *Mark a 2 on the city when you get there.*

Nora had a grand time, although the city is bigger and busier than anyplace she'd ever been before. It is right on the harbor, so big ships come there. Nora watched them unload things from all over the world. *Draw a big ship in the harbor and mark it 3.*

"I've had enough of all this noise," Nora thought. "I'd like to find a quiet spot where I can take a nap and dream of bones or something nice like that." From a tall building, she could see an island out in the ocean. It looked very quiet. Nora is a good swimmer, so she paddled out to the island and took a nap. Sure enough, she had a very large bone in her dream. *Draw a line to the island and put a 4 on it.*

Now that Nora was rested, she was ready to see something new. "I've never seen anyone skiing," she thought. "I'll go to the mountains." When Nora got back to dry land, she decided to follow the river to the mountains. She knew that skiing started there. She walked along the river, around the lake, and through the valley. *Follow Nora's path and mark a 5 on the river.* This was flat land—easy walking.

Now Nora started climbing. "Whew," she thought," this is hard work." The land was steep and there weren't many towns where she could stop for a bone or two. However, Nora really wanted to see the skiers, so she kept on climbing. Finally, she reached the top of the highest mountain and there were the skiers. *Draw Nora's route and mark a 6 at the top of the highest mountain.*

Nora couldn't find any skis to fit her, so she just slid down the mountain on her paws. "I'm a little chilly. I think it's time to go home now," Nora thought when she picked herself up and brushed off the snow. *Find the easiest way for Nora to get back to Geotown. Mark the way and draw a bone on Geotown.*

2. Use Reproducible 25 and/or the poster as the basis for further discussion of the best geographical location for various human activities. Ask the children where they think a very large ship would go and where it would be safe to be in a very small boat. Discuss where they could fish, and where they could do some climbing Then ask the children to think about why the biggest city in the picture is where it is and why it might be on the water instead of where Geotown is. Discuss why the city is on flat land instead of high in the mountains. Why is the farm on flat land too?

Across The Curriculum

Linking Art And Geography

Children can build three-dimensional models from clay or playdough of the Geotown area using Reproducible 25 and/or the poster as a model. Some may prefer to model their own area or a place they'd like to visit. They may even include troughs for rivers so that they can demonstrate water flowing from the high mountain areas down to the coastal plain.

Linking Literature And Geography

There are many wonderful books in which geographic features play a major role. You might supply a variety of these storybooks for children to browse through and choose a favorite. Some are particularly good for reading aloud to the class. Ask each child to tell how the landforms or bodies of water in the story affected the characters, and vice versa. Books to consider

Mifflin), *Where the Forest Meets the Sea* by Jeannie Baker (Greenwillow Books), *When I Was Young in the Mountains* by Cynthia Rylant (Dutton), and *Sarah, Plain and Tall* by Patricia MacLachlan (HarperCollins).

Linking Writing And Geography

I Am the Ocean by Suzanna Marshak (Little, Brown) gives children a broad picture of the incredible variety of life in the ocean. Encourage them to choose landforms to read about and describe in "I Am..." stories of their own. Be sure they include how their landforms affect the people who live near them.

Linking Science And Geography

Using Lisa Westburg Peters' book *The Sun, the Wind, and the Rain* (Henry Holt), explore with children how mountains were formed. If a sand table is available, let children experiment with some of Peters' analogies between a child's playing in the sand and the creation of mountains.

IT'S RAINING, IT'S POURING
Learning About Climate

Good weather, bad weather, freak weather; day in, and day out, there is always some kind of weather and it affects us all. To wake up to a warm, sunny day with just a hint of a breeze is very different from waking up to a freezing sleeting, windy day. And just as weather may affect children's plans for the day, climate affects the plans of much larger groups of people or cultures. Today's media-blitzed children have been exposed on television and in movies to many different climates and the cultures that have adapted to them. These activities will help them to organize the information they have and use it to analyze their own climate.

Differentiating Among The Four Seasons

Children already know a great deal about weather and climate and its effects on their lives. Help them organize that prior knowledge to better understand cause-and-effect relationships.

Materials Needed

1. Outdoor thermometer

2. Chart paper

3. Travel magazines

4. Paste

5. Scissors

Before Starting

Place the outdoor thermometer in a place where children can read it easily.

What To Do

1. Start the discussion by encouraging the children to talk about the weather today. Accept all descriptions offered. Help children see that their weather descriptions involve temperature, precipitation, and wind.

2. Have a volunteer read the outdoor thermometer to find the actual temperature at the moment. Invite the children to recall the various kinds of precipitation they have seen, and to tell stories that they have heard or experienced of the effects of the wind.

3. Write the words *weather* and *climate* on the board. Explain that weather means whether it is hot or cold, rainy or clear, windy or still on any given day. Climate refers to the weather over a long period of time. You may want to write *today* next to *weather* and *long time* next to *climate*.

4. Have the children make a climate chart for their area. Ask them to name the four seasons as you write each one on the chart, leaving room for descriptions of the climate. As the children suggest typical weather conditions in each season, list them under the appropriate heading. Point out that they know a lot about climate, because all of this information together describes their area's climate. If there are children who have lived in or visited a place with a very different climate, they can compare and contrast it with that of their present community.

5. Have children describe what they wear in each of the seasons and discuss how this relates to the climate. Select different items they have described and ask if, and why or why not, they would wear this in another season. Children who have lived in very different climates can describe how their clothing differed. You may want to make a chart for each season and let children draw pictures of the clothing they wear in each.

6. Ask the children to think of some things that they do in one kind of weather that they don't do in others. The discussion can range from clear cause-and-effect situations such as not having a picnic in the rain, to more sophisticated relationships such as what you eat in certain seasons. For example, they probably eat corn in the summertime when it has warm weather in which to grow. Again, you may wish to make a chart to help children categorize the activities according to the seasons.

Across The Curriculum

Linking Creative Dramatics And Geography

Have volunteers pantomime seasonal activities and have other children identify the activity and the season. Encourage them to give reasons why this season is best for the activity.

Linking Language And Geography

Make word webs for different kinds of weather, like rain, sunshine, snow, or for different seasons. Then let children use the subsequent word banks for "I like/I hate" sentences. Tell the class that some scary stories begin with "It was a dark and rainy night…" and discuss how weather words make us feel. This could lead to children writing short poems that express their feelings about weather or seasons.

Recording Weather Over A Long Period Of Time

The recording of weather will be most useful—and most fun—if it is done over the period of several months, or even the entire school year.

Materials Needed

1. Reproducibles 28 (p. 108) and 29 (p. 109)

2. Large outdoor thermometer

3. 6 permanent markers (preferably purple, blue, green, yellow, orange, and red)

4. Chart paper

5. Paste

Before Starting

1. Color code the outdoor thermometer with permanent markers as follows: below 15°–no color, 15° to 32°–purple, 32° to 45°–blue, 45° to 60°–green, 60° to 75°–yellow, 75° to 90°–orange, and above 90°–red. Place the thermometer in a spot where children can read it easily.

2. Using the same markers, make a color bar across the bottom of each temperature card from Reproducible 28 as follows: very frigid - no color, frigid - purple, cold - blue, cool - green, warm - yellow, hot - orange, and very hot - red. Cut out several sets of the cards.

3. Set up a weather chart titled with the month and the name of your community. List the days of the current month with space for two cards beside each day.

What To Do

1. Appoint two or three children to take turns being meteorologists. At the same time every day, they will read the thermometer and observe the other weather conditions. They will then select and paste on the chart the best temperature and weather cards from those provided on Reproducibles 28 and 29.

2. Periodically, have the children compare the weather from month to month to get an accurate picture of the climate. At the end of the school year, they can identify the coldest, hottest, rainiest, and sunniest months.

This activity results in a dramatic monthly bar graph that gives a profile of the community's temperatures.

January in Geotown

S	M	T	W	T	F	S
					1	2
3	4	5	6	7	8	9
10	11	12	13	14	15	16
17	18	19	20	21	22	23
24	25	26	27	28	29	30

Graphing Temperatures

Materials Needed

1. Reproducible 30 (p. 110)

2. 6 markers to match thermometer colors (see the preceding activity)

3. Outdoor thermometer

Before Starting

If it is not already marked, color code the outdoor thermometer as described in the preceding activity.

What To Do

1. Assign a child or pair of children to observe the thermometer, choose the matching colored marker, and color the correct box of the bar graph provided on Reproducible 30.

2. Use a separate graph for each month. At the end of the school year, encourage the children to compare the bar graphs from different months and to make generalizations about the community's climate. They might ask grandparents or senior citizens in the community whether the climate has changed over the years.

Across The Curriculum

Linking Literature And Geography

Bringing the Rain to Kapiti Plain by Verna Aardema (Dial) is a retelling on a traditional Kenyan tale of drought. Have children describe the weather in the story and imagine what would happen in their community if the weather was like this.

Linking Creative Dramatics And Geography

Help children learn how to read the weather map in your local newspaper. If there are a few "hams" in the class, let them act as TV weather reporters using the newspaper weather maps as their visual props. Encourage the "reporters" to use as many descriptive phrases as they can in imitating the often extravagant language of TV weather reports. You might also try to videotape television weather spots and review them with the class.

OUR TOWN
Making A Model Community

One of the most exciting and ambitious projects for young geographers is to build a model of their own community. It draws on all the geographic skills children have learned, from creating symbols and finding directions to calculating distance and scale. More than that, looking back and forth from the model to the map will help develop the spatial skills required to visualize a place from a map. It is this ability that will truly qualify children as map literate and enable them to enjoy reading maps for the rest of their lives.

Making The Model

Materials Needed

1. Local map
2. Collection of boxes, milk cartons, cans, blocks of wood, and other objects to serve as buildings
3. Paper and other materials to create fronts of buildings
4. Cardboard or plywood (for map base)
5. Paints, crayons, markers
6. Scissors
7. Paste and tape
8. Yarn, cotton balls, and small sticks (optional)

Before Starting

1. The largest-scale map you can find will be the easiest to use for this activity. The map should locate important local buildings and sites. It

might also be helpful to have a smaller-scale map of the community for general reference. If possible, have an overhead transparency made of this map so that you can project it and discuss it with the entire class.

2. A great deal of planning needs to take place before the actual model is constructed. The more you involve the children in this process, the better. This will be a wonderful opportunity for you and the children to solve problems together. Don't hesitate to pose problems that you don't have an answer to, and let the children be part of solving them.

3. If for some reason it is impractical to make a model of their own community, let the children make a model of Geotown. The views and maps on both sides of the poster provide ample reference material.

What To Do

1. Decide how large your model is going to be. Its size will be based on the amount of space that you wish to occupy with the model. There are so many activities children can do using the model, that it would be beneficial to display it for awhile. (One teacher we know involved the whole school in the project, creating the model in the school gym.)

2. With size in mind, determine the area that you are going to model—a part of the community, the whole community, or the community and its outskirts. Mark that area on your local map.

3. Decide on the scale to be used. You may want to do this mathematically or informally by counting neighborhood blocks. Your calculations will be based on the overall size of the model. For example, if your model is 20 inches wide and you want to show 10 blocks, each block will be 2 inches long.

4. Lay out a surface for the map base. It can be made of cardboard or thin plywood if the model needs to be picked up for storage.

When you are positioning the base, don't forget to orient the model correctly so that north in the model faces north in the classroom. Mark the directions on the model in some way.

5. You will probably need to sketch out the streets, avenues, rivers, and other base guidelines from a map, but the children should be part of the process. Have them read the map and act as advisors. Work in pencil or chalk because the areas may have to be adjusted later when the buildings are added.

6. Decide on guidelines for buildings to be shown in the model. Since it will be impossible to show every single house or structure on the model, make a plan with the children for what to include. For example, you might select important community buildings and landmarks to construct and show all other buildings with colored squares on the base of the model. Mark on your local map the locations of all of the buildings and sites you are going to represent in the model.

7. Decide with the children how the buildings are to be constructed. They can paint blocks of wood, wrap cans and cartons in paper, or even make buildings out of folded paper colored with crayons. Students can work in teams making the buildings for a whole block or area, or they can work individually on one building at a time. As buildings are completed, they can be placed on the model base. However, do not paste them down yet.

8. When all the buildings are completed, make whatever adjustments are necessary to the map base. Then remove the buildings and let the children decide on what colors to paint the streets, avenues, parking lots, waterways, parks, woods, fields, empty lots, and so on.

9. After the children have painted all the two-dimensional sites, place the buildings back on the model and paste them down. Let the children add whatever finishing touches their imaginations inspire, that is, trees, grass, fish, swans on a lake, cars on the streets, street signs—whatever miniature creations they like.

Across The Curriculum

Linking Writing And Geography

Have the children write invitations to the unveiling of their community model. They might consider inviting other classes, parents, school and local officials, and all those who donated materials to the project. Have the children summarize how they made the model or help them write a description of the activity to hand out to visitors.

Linking Literature And Geography

What's in a Map by Sally Cartwright (Putnam) would be interesting for children to study at this point. Cartwright uses sand and block maps to help children understand geographical relationships.

Using The Model

Once the model has been created, it can be the setting for a wide range of geographic inquiries. What follows is only a partial list of the kinds of questions you can explore with the children using the model.

Materials Needed

1. Model of the community prepared in previous activity

What To Do

1. Exploration of WHERE: Have the children analyze the parts of their community. Where are the residential areas? The shopping areas? The parks and recreation areas? Hospitals? Fire stations? Schools? Churches?

2. Exploration of WHY: Can the children see any reasons why a fire station is located where it is or why a particular mall was built in its present location? Were they always there? Have buildings been moved, and why?

3. Exploration of HOW: Have children use the model to show routes, such as, the way they come to school, the way they go to the park, and the way their parents go to work. Have them talk about who they see when they go places. Which areas of the community are the busiest and which are the quietest? How does this vary depending on the time of day?

4. Exploration of PLACE: Ask each child to point to his or her favorite place in the community and explain why it is special. They will want to identify the approximate places where their homes are located.

5. Exploration of POTENTIAL: Discuss what children would like to change in the community. What would they like to add to the community? What would they like to take away? What would they like to fix. Encourage the children to compare and contrast their community to Geotown.

Exploring Types Of Communities

Materials Needed

1. Poster

2. Reproducibles 31 (p. 111) and 32 (p. 112)

3. Model of the community prepared earlier.

What To Do

1. Have the children describe each of the pictures from Reproducibles 31 and 32. List these descriptions on the board. For example, for picture 4 you may write "few buildings," "lots of farmland," and so on. Word webs will help you organize these descriptions.

2. Next ask children to make comparisons. How do the buildings differ in each place? What would they do in each place? Where would they prefer to live?

3. Finally, ask children if your community looks like any of these places. Have them identify similarities and differences.

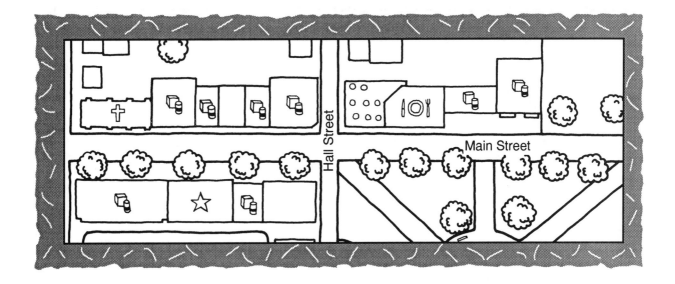

GETTING DOWN TO BUSINESS
Learning About Economic Geography

Try these activities with your children and you may find the economic geographers of the future.

Choosing A Site For A Business

While considering the hands-on problem of finding the best place to locate a lemonade stand, your young geographers will choose a location by analyzing probable movement patterns, needs of the population, and location of competitors.

Materials Needed

1. Poster (Side 2)

2. Reproducible 33 (p. 113)

3. Model of lemonade stand from Reproducible 5 (p.85)

4. Model of the community prepared in previous activity (pp. 67-68)

What To Do

1. Read the following story to the class. As each location is named, have the children find it on the Geotown map on copies of Reproducible 33.

Zoe and Tad and Their Lemonade Stand

Zoe and Tad wanted to raise money to buy a rabbit for their classroom. It was September, but it was so hot that it felt like the middle of summer. They thought of raking leaves but there weren't any on the ground yet. They were still trying to think when Zoe's mom asked, "Would you like some nice cold lemonade?"

"That's it." they both cried at once. "We can sell lemonade. Let's start right now." And so they did.

In front of Zoe's house on Hall Street, they put out a little stool with the lemonade, some paper cups, and a sign that read "Lemonade, 25¢ a Cup". [*Allow the children enough time to locate Zoe's house on Hall Street.*] It was a nice quiet spot under a tree. All they had to do was wait for their first customer. They waited, and waited, and waited. And as they waited they began to wonder what was wrong with their idea. *Why do you think nobody came?* That is what Zoe and Tad soon realized. It was not the idea that was bad, but the place. So, they decided to move their stand to Bridge Street. There was always a lot of traffic there. *Find Bridge Street and mark a spot where Zoe and Tad might have put their stand.*

On Bridge Street, they set up their lemonade stand again with high hopes, as one car after another whizzed by. The light turned red and the cars stopped. Then, some turned right, while others sat there staring at the light, ready to go the second the light turned green again. When it did, the cars rushed by in a blur. Then the light turned red again, then green again, then red, then green.... What was wrong this time? It was a hot day and there was lots of traffic. *What was wrong with having the stand on Bridge Street?*

That is just what Zoe and Tad soon realized. There was too much traffic and it was going too fast. What they needed was a spot where people moved slowly. People walking would be best for their lemonade business. "We should go to Main Street," Zoe said. "That's where people walk around, and that's why all the stores are there."

So off they went to set up their stand on Main Street, right in front of Joe's Busy Corner. *Find Joe's on Main Street and mark a spot where the lemonade stand can be.* Sure enough, Mr. Chen stopped for a glass on his way into the store. When Mrs. Pink and her daughter saw Mr. Chen's lemonade, they rushed out of Joe's to get some too.

Pretty soon Joe himself followed people out of the store to see where all of his customers were going. When he saw the lemonade stand, he grew red in the face. He started sputtering and muttering. "Twenty-five cents!" they heard him grumble. "Twenty-five cents!" He grew louder and madder. He was beside himself. His store had to pay taxes and rent and a whole lot of bills. To make a profit, Joe had to sell his lemonade for 50¢ a glass. Joe caught his breath and his temper and he explained to Zoe and Tad, as nicely as he could, that they had to move. "You cannot sell lemonade in front of my store," he explained.

Poor Zoe, poor Tad. Where could they go? *Can anyone explain why Joe asked Zoe and Tad to leave? Can anyone find a good place in Geotown for the lemonade stand? Someplace where there are lots of people who are walking, no one is driving fast, and there are no shopkeepers to upset.*

2. Discuss possible locations with the children, using the poster and the map on Reproducible 33. Good locations might be in the park or near the school or the library. Let children mark the spots they choose on their copy of the reproducible.

3. Let the children debate where to put a lemonade stand in their community. They can make a small stand using the cutout on Reproducible 5 and place it on their community model. You may want to carry this activity even further by asking the children to think of actual businesses that they would like to open. Have them decide where to place their businesses in their community and explain the reasons why they chose their locations. If they wish, children can add their new businesses to the community model.

Across The Curriculum

Linking Economics And Geography

Children can set up lemonade stands at school to raise money for a chosen cause. First, they will need to agree on a price for a cup of lemonade. Then, working in teams, the children will select locations, set up the stands, make the lemonade, and do the actual selling. When the sales of all of the stands are compared, children can discuss the variables that affected sales.

LONG LONG AGO
Learning About Historical Geography

How much historical geography do your students know? Probably quite a bit, although they haven't identified it as such. Every child raised with American television has seen, for example, cattle drives in the Old West. What they have seen on those programs is what the West was like before the invention of barbed wire. Understanding how places change and the role geography has in that change is what historical geographers do. In this section, children will look at the historical geography of Geotown and their own community.

Discovering The History Of Geotown

These activities will allow the children to investigate community changes and will introduce them to the great movements of American history.

Materials Needed
. . . .
1. Poster (Side 2)

2. Reproducibles 34 (p. 114), 35 (p. 115), 36 (p. 116), and 37 (p. 117)

3. Calculator tape or computer paper

Note: The four pictures presented on Reproducibles 34, 35, 36, and 37 show the site of Geotown and its changes over the course of hundreds of years. Encourage the children to compare and contrast them to see the different ways that people have used the land and been affected by the land over time.

What To Do

1. Ask the class who lived where you live hundreds and hundreds of years ago. Who were the very first people who lived here? Tell them something about the first Americans who lived in your area.

2. Distribute copies of Reproducible 34 and introduce the picture as the site of Geotown, shown hundreds of years ago. Ask the children who they think lived here and tell them that this group of Native Americans were called *Commanche*. Discuss the picture and encourage children to describe the landforms, using the correct terms. Pose questions about why the Native Americans might have chosen to settle in this place. (The hills were a source for wood, the plains for buffalo, the river for water and fish and so on.)

3. Distribute copies of Reproducible 35. Once the children have discovered that this is a picture of the same place, ask them why they think this is true. Have the children put the two pictures in chronological order and describe the changes that have occurred. (There are no more buffalo and fewer trees. There is a wagon road. On the nearby hills there are fewer trees. Water is diverted from the river for gardens, and so on. This is the beginning of Geotown.)

4. Distribute copies of Reproducible 36. Ask children what features they can find on Reproducible 36 that are in the picture of Geotown on the Poster (Side 2).Have the children add this picture to the other two and arrange them in correct order. Invite them to identify what has happened to the community and the landforms since the last picture. (The railroad has come. The river has been dammed and water has been diverted for farms. There are plowed fields. The hills are bare of trees. The town has grown.) You may also want the children to identify the things on this picture that have stayed the same from the last picture (the geographical features.)

5. Finally, distribute copies of Reproducible 37. The children will probably recognize this as a picture of Geotown today. Ask them to put the four pictures in order and to describe the changes that have happened to the place between long ago and today. Discuss things that stayed the same over the years.

Across The Curriculum

Linking Literature And Geography

When told with stories and illustrations, the history of the interaction between humans and the environment is exciting and understandable for primary children. Some books that accomplish this are: *Heron Street* by Ann Turner (HarperCollins), *The Little House* by Virginia Lee Burton (Houghton Mifflin), *New Providence: A Changing Cityscape* by Renata von Tscharner and Robert Lee Fleming (Harcourt Brace), *Forest, Village, Town, City* by Dan Beekman (Thomas Y. Crowell), and *A River Ran Wild* by Lynn Cherry (Harcourt Brace).

Linking Writing And Geography

Children can choose the time they would like to have lived in Geotown and tell why. They may want to write stories about living in Geotown long ago. These stories will be enriched if the children have read some of the books noted above.

Discovering The History Of Your Community

Materials Needed

1. Pictures of your community from the past

2. Model of the community prepared in previous activity (p. 67-68)

Before Starting

1. Find out which Native American groups lived in your area long ago. Try to obtain materials on these groups that are appropriate for children. Your local or state historical society may be able to supply this information. (If pictures specific to your community are not available, use several pictures of the group or groups who first lived in your area.)

2. Gather a selection of pictures of the community from the past. Your best sources probably will be the local library, museums, historical societies, and local newspapers. Other sources include the town hall, chamber of commerce, local fraternal organizations, or sometimes even the public relations departments of leading industries. If pictures specific to the community are not available, use general pictures of the area.

3. You may also want to locate people in the community who are knowledgeable about its history and arrange for some of them to speak to the children.

What To Do

1. Allow the children to browse through the pictures and put them in chronological order. It might be helpful to group the pictures into broad categories such as "When the First People Lived Here," "When Our Town Was Born a Hundred Years Ago," and so on. As children study the pictures, encourage them to look for geographic features that have changed, like forests or grasslands that have disappeared, and those that have stayed the same, such as a mountain or lake that looks the same over time.

2. Help the children investigate the history of their community through whatever books,

exhibits, and speakers are available and appropriate for children of their age. Encourage the children to show what they have learned about their community by drawing pictures, creating models or dioramas, making up stories about their favorite times to have lived in, and so on.

3. Have children study the model they made of their community and discuss what features would have been there a hundred years ago.

4. Help the children make a timeline showing major events in their community history. You can use continuous computer paper or calculator tape. Be sure to include on your timeline happenings that are related to geographic features, such as when a lake was dammed or when a famous tree was cut down.

5. If possible, invite an older citizen who has lived in the community to describe how the community has changed in his or her lifetime. You may want to arrange for the children to visit a nearby retirement community or nursing home so they can hear about their community as it used to be.

Across The Curriculum

Linking Writing And Geography

Allow children to choose the time they would like to have lived in your community. Have them select the pictures for their period. Ask them to write a description of that time based on the pictures. When the histories are finished, have the groups select a representative to read them in chronological order.

DREAMTOWN
Learning About Urban Geography

Natural occurences cause environmental changes, like volcanoes, storms, earthquakes, droughts, and floods. However, most changes to the environment today are caused by human activity. Just as it is people who may have made places unhealthy, dangerous, dull, or ugly, it is people who can make their environment more healthy, safe, interesting, and beautiful. The most important lesson for your young geographers is that it is they who must plan for the future. With this activity they can become city planners and environmental geographers. We hope that, what they plan for Geotown, they may one day achieve in their own communities.

Planning For Geotown's Future

Materials Needed

1. Poster (Side 2, Band A)

2. Reproducibles 38 (p. 118) and 39 (p. 119)

3. Crayons or colored pencils

4. Scissors

5. Paste

What To Do

1. Tell the class that they are going to be city planners for Geotown. They have the power to decide what is going to happen in the future—a park along the river, a playground for little children near their homes, a civic

center, recycling centers, a children's library near the school, and a Geotown Museum.

2. Choose one of the places pictured on Reproducibles 38 and 39—the park, for example. Let the class discuss where to put a new park in Geotown. If there is disagreement, have the class vote, just as the citizens of Geotown would. You may suggest that they need to "tear down" some of the buildings by covering them with the new ones. Be sure that the children have plenty of opportunity to explain why they chose the location they did.

3. Discuss with the class what they like in their own community, what they don't like, and the changes that could be made to make it a healthier, safer, more beautiful, and a more interesting place to live. Ask children to draw pictures of their ideas.

Across The Curriculum

Linking Writing And Geography.

Invite the children to write letters to the mayor or the city council explaining their ideas to better the community. You may want to send the letters and the pictures to the office of the mayor, the city council, or to the local newspaper.

A Geography Network

Geography teaching in the United States is thriving and you can be an active part of its growth. The Geographic Alliance Network is a state-based network of about 100,000 educators (kindergarten through grade twelve teachers and university professors) who share ideas and learn together. Each state's alliance is based in a university within the state. To find out about the Geographic Alliance in your state, write to:

Geographic Education Program

National Geographic Society

1145 17th Street NW

Washington, D.C. 20036

You and your young geographers have begun an exciting adventure. Looking at the world through geographers' eyes is an endlessly fascinating experience. Have a great trip!

Reproducibles

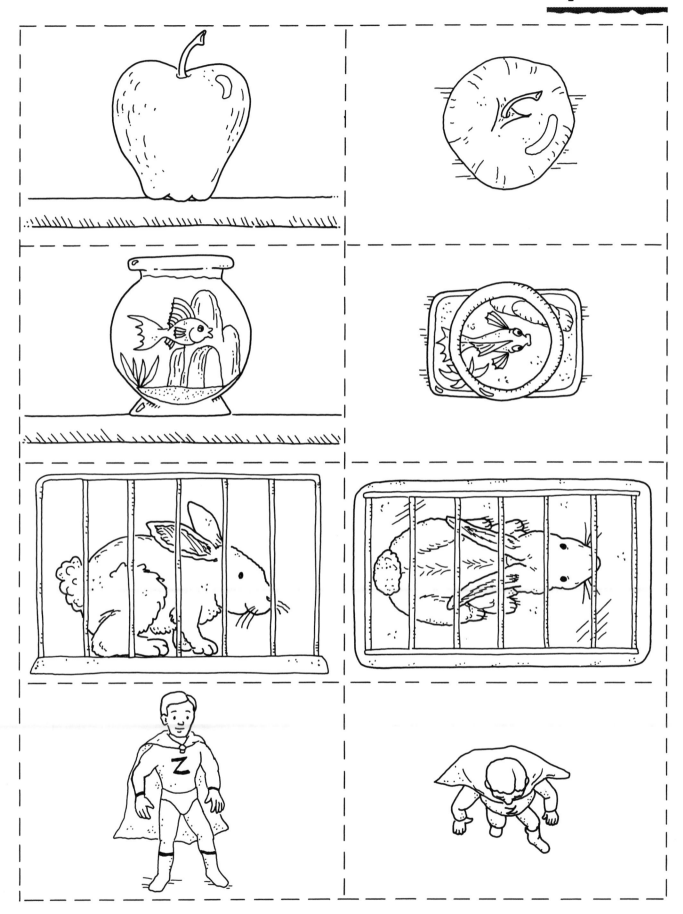

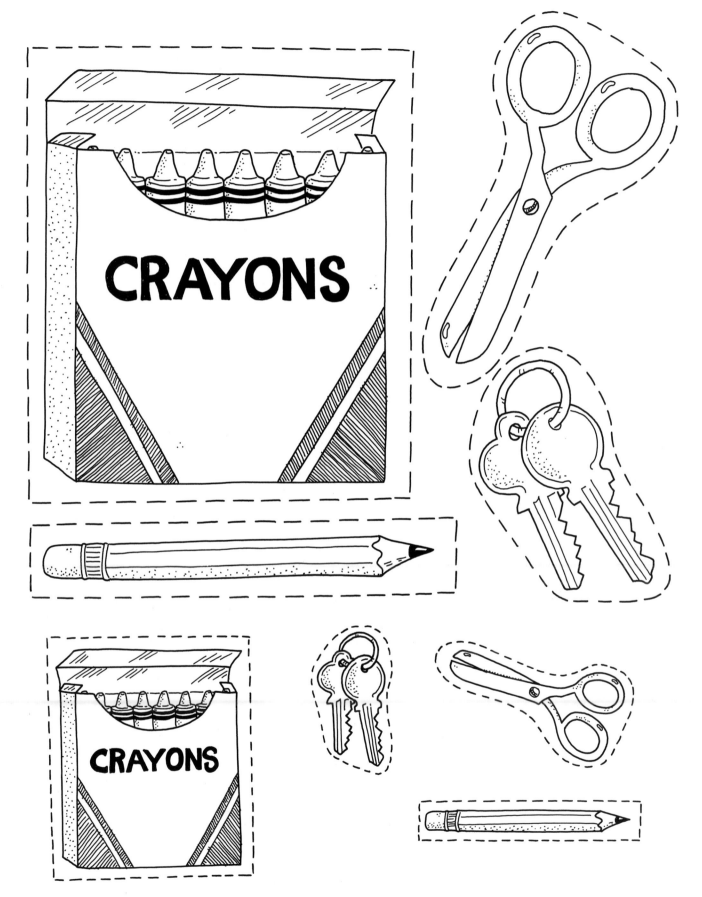

Reproducible 4

1	2	3
4	5	6
7	8	9

Full scale

Small scale

1	2	3
4	5	6
7	8	9

Fold on the double lines.

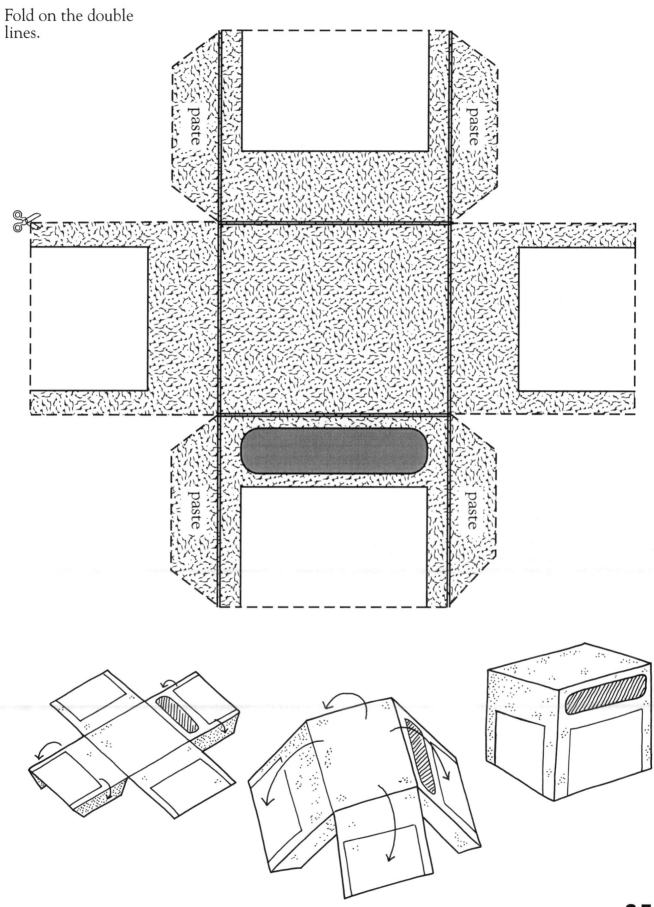

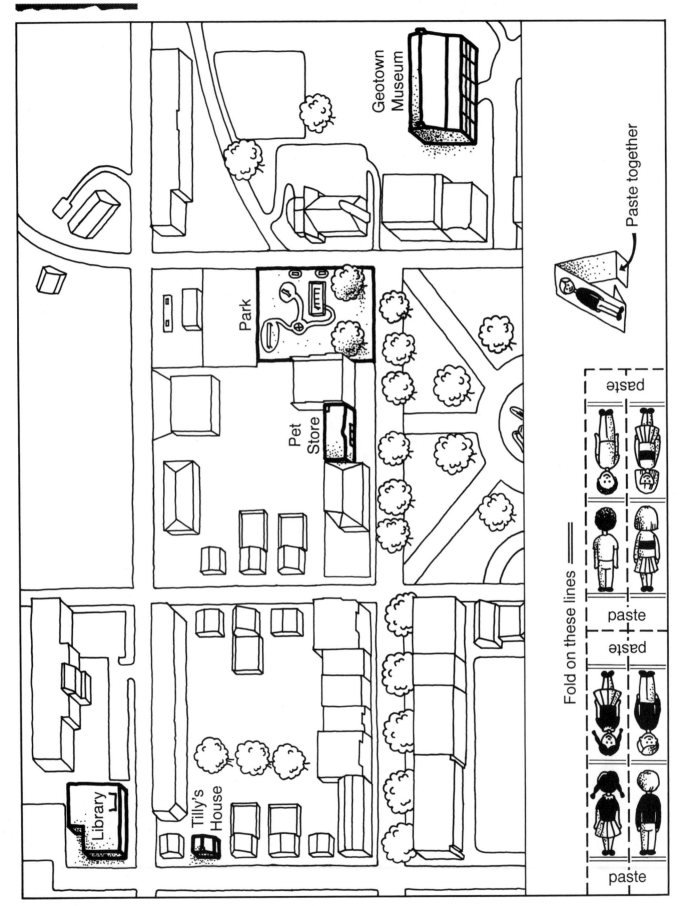

Geotown Museum

Park

Pet Store

Library

Tilly's House

Paste together

Fold on these lines

paste

paste

paste

paste

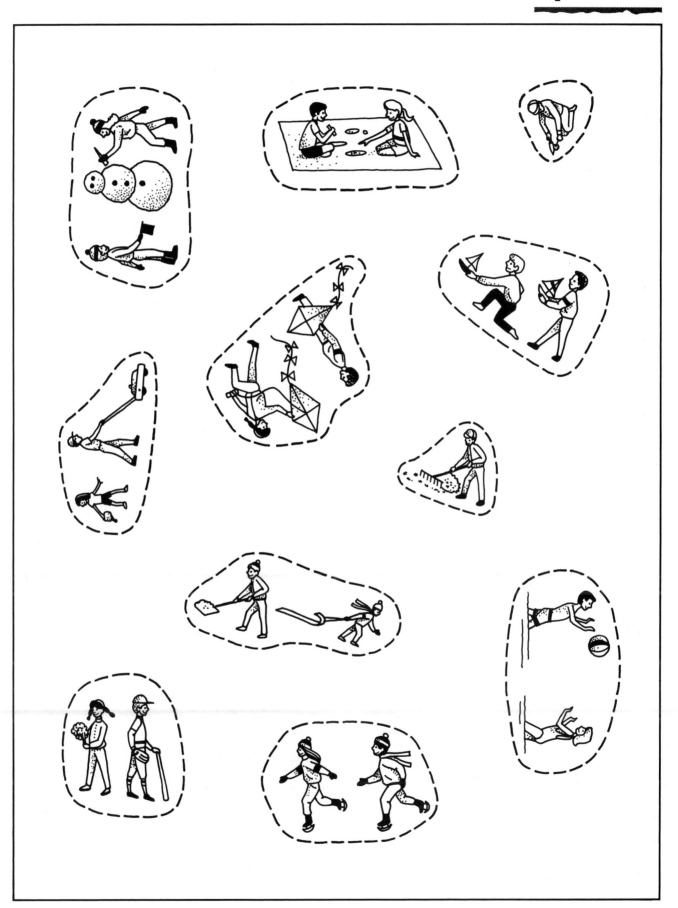

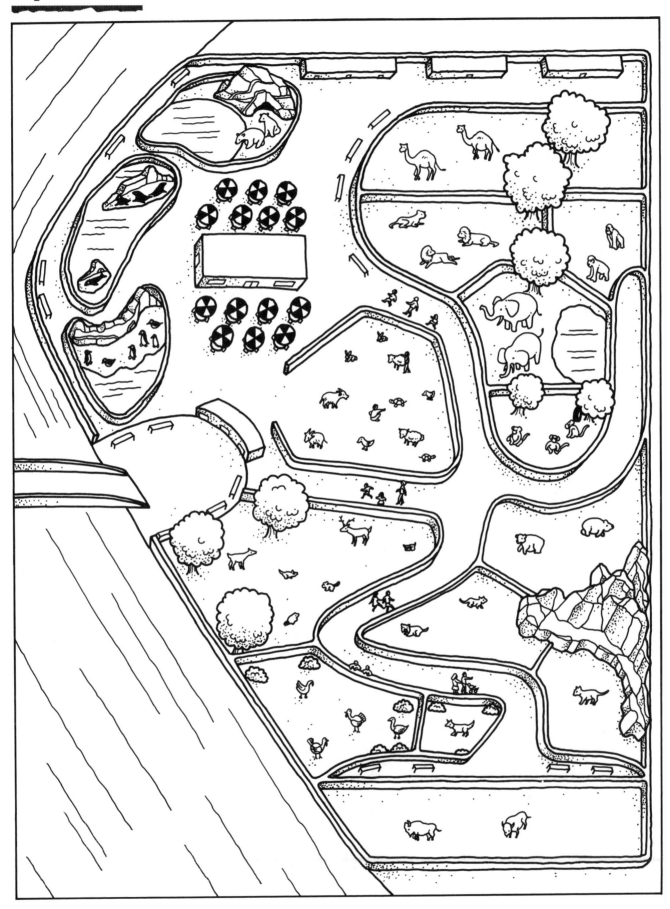

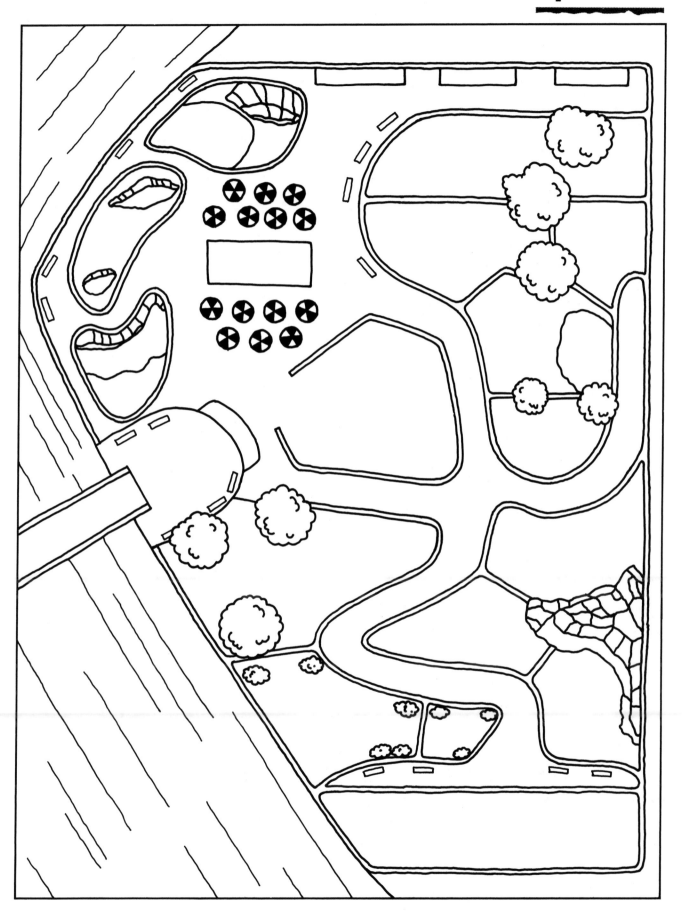

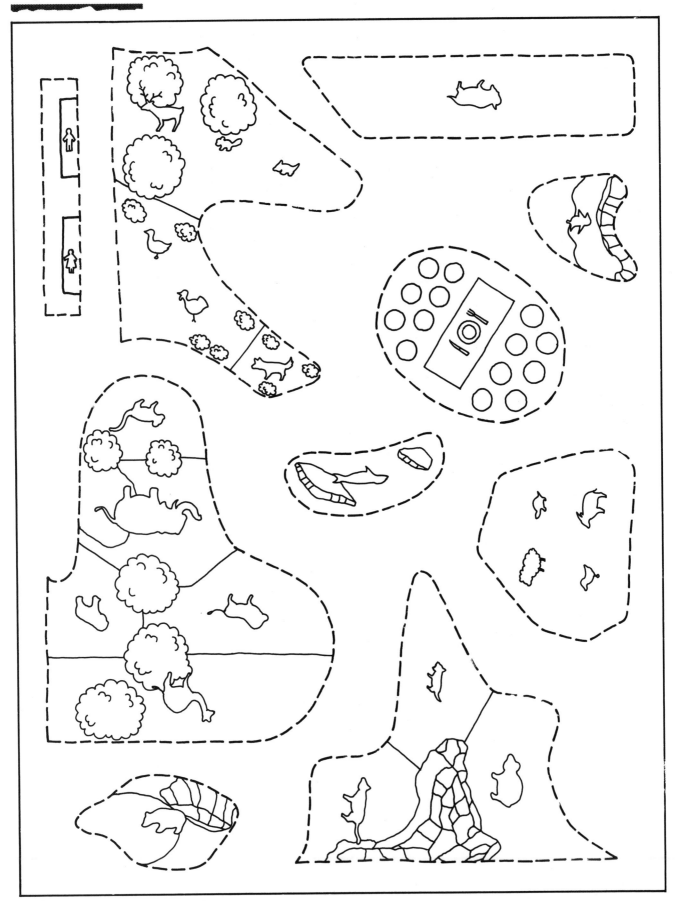

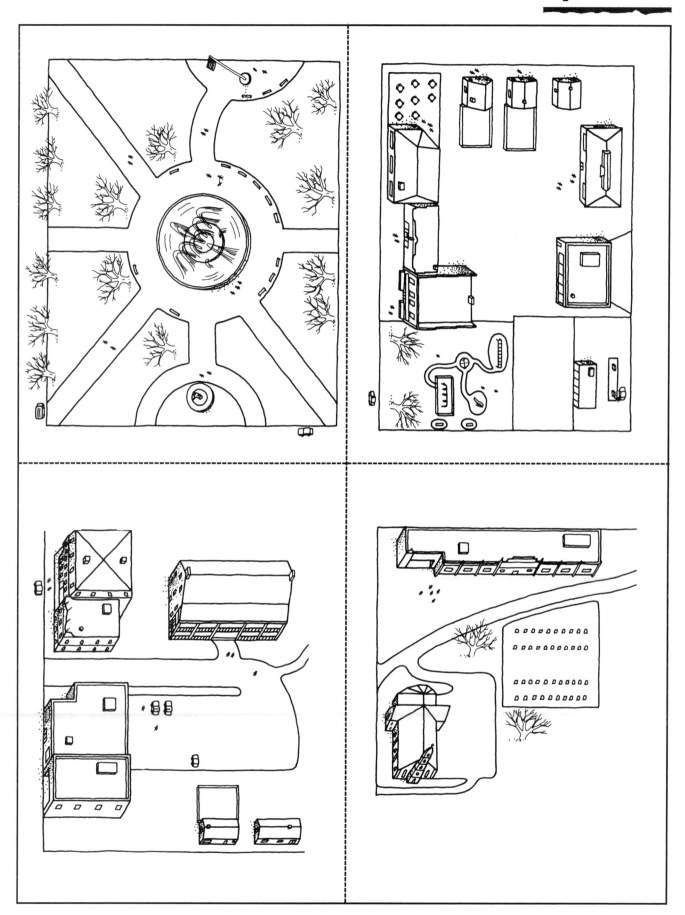

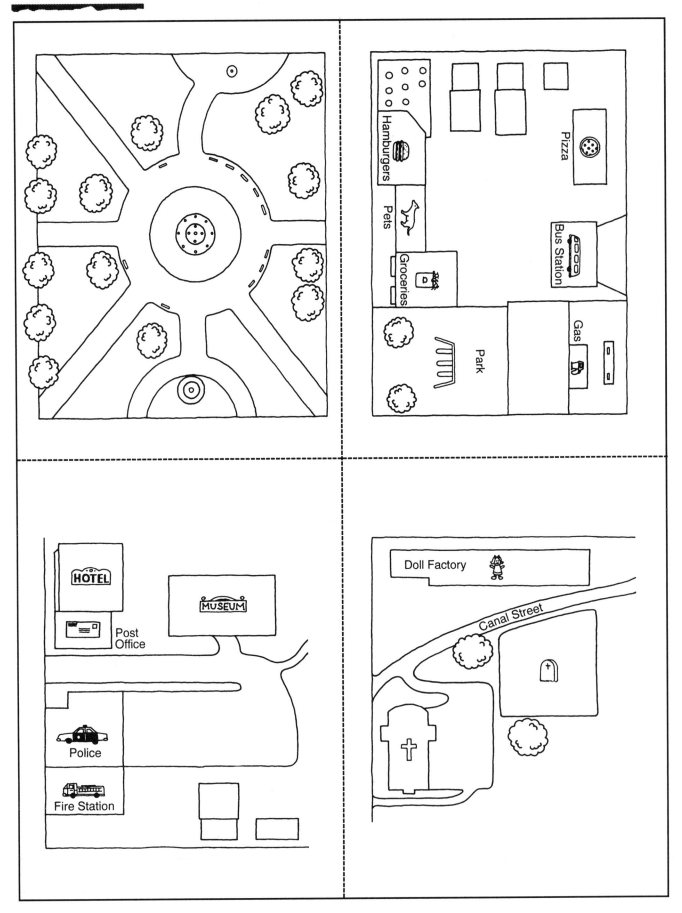

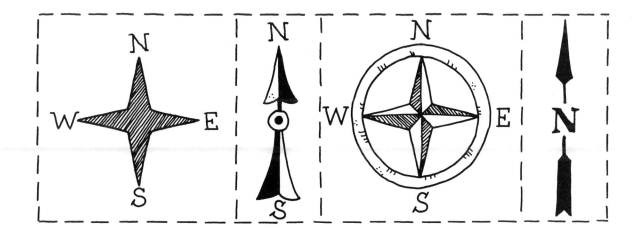

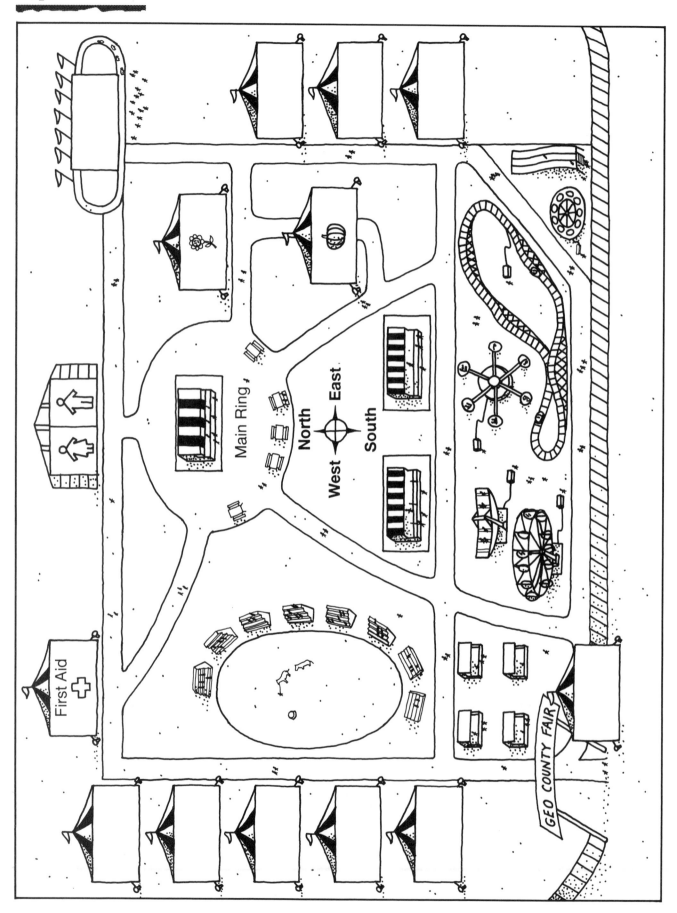

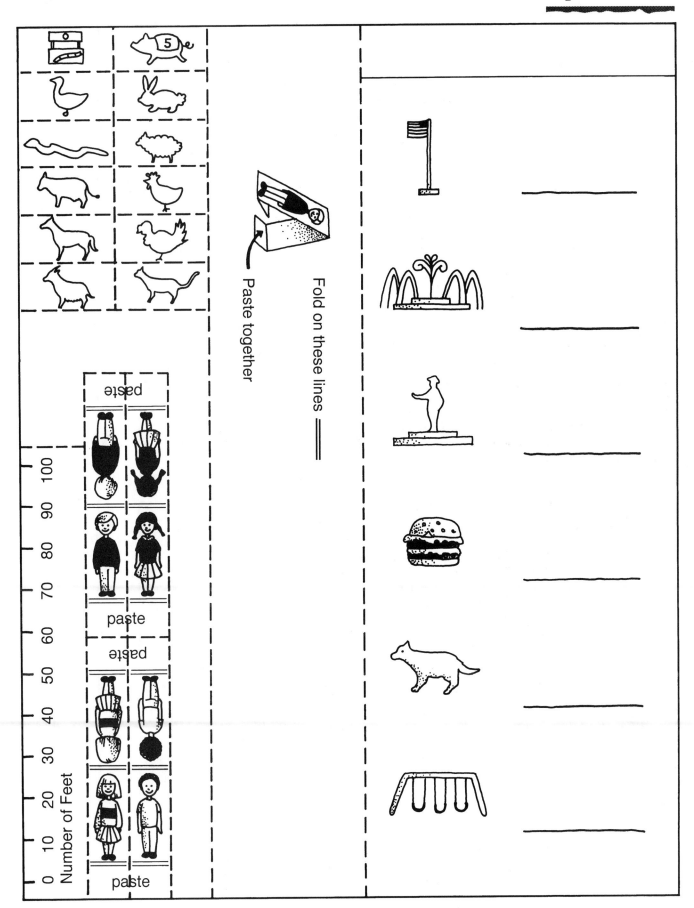

Paste together

Fold on these lines ══

paste

paste

paste

paste

Number of Feet
0 10 20 30 40 50 60 70 80 90 100

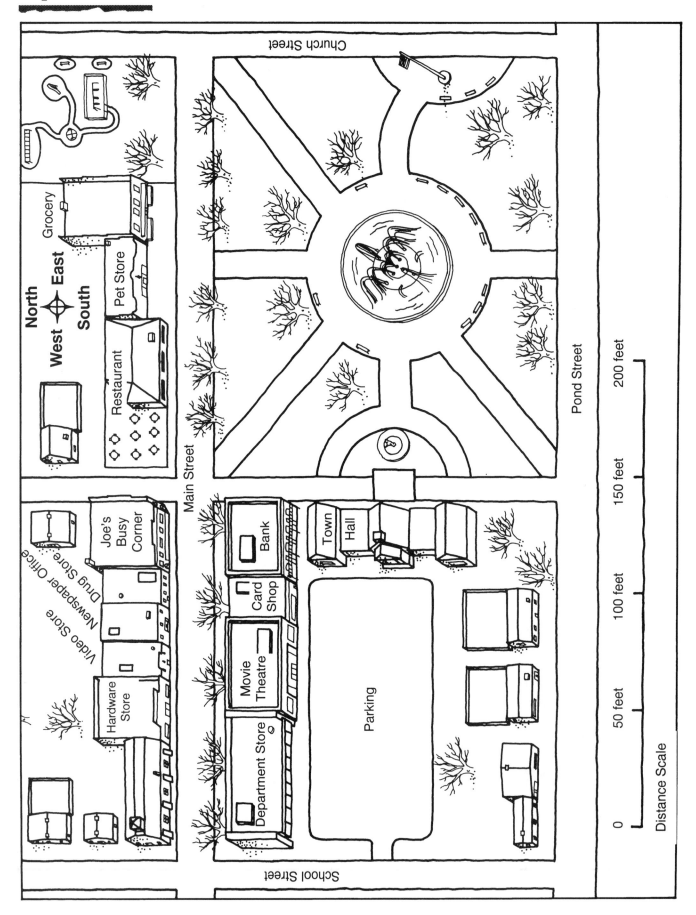

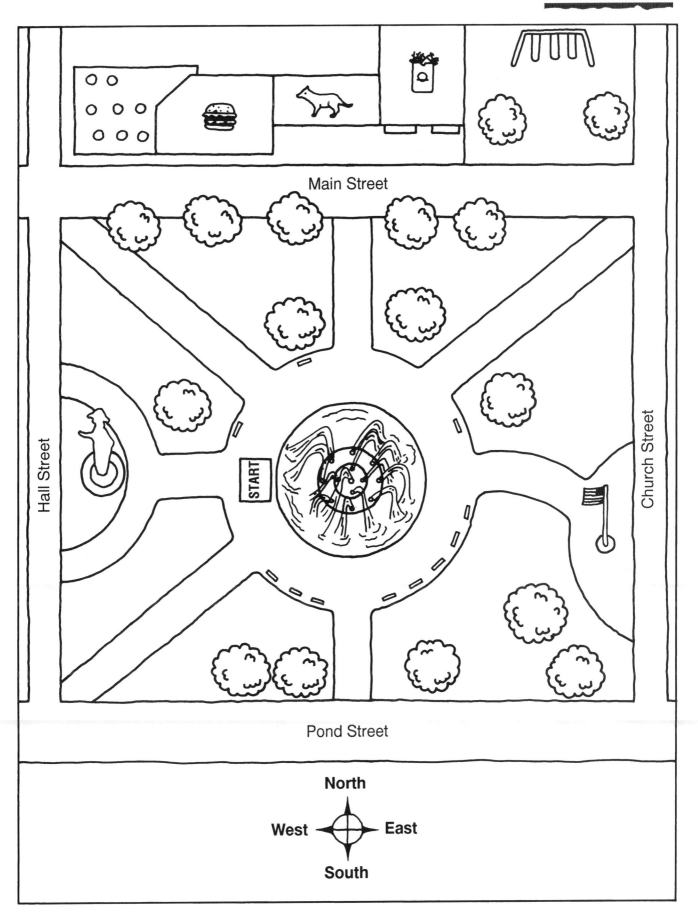

Main Street

Hall Street

Church Street

START

Pond Street

North

West ✦ **East**

South

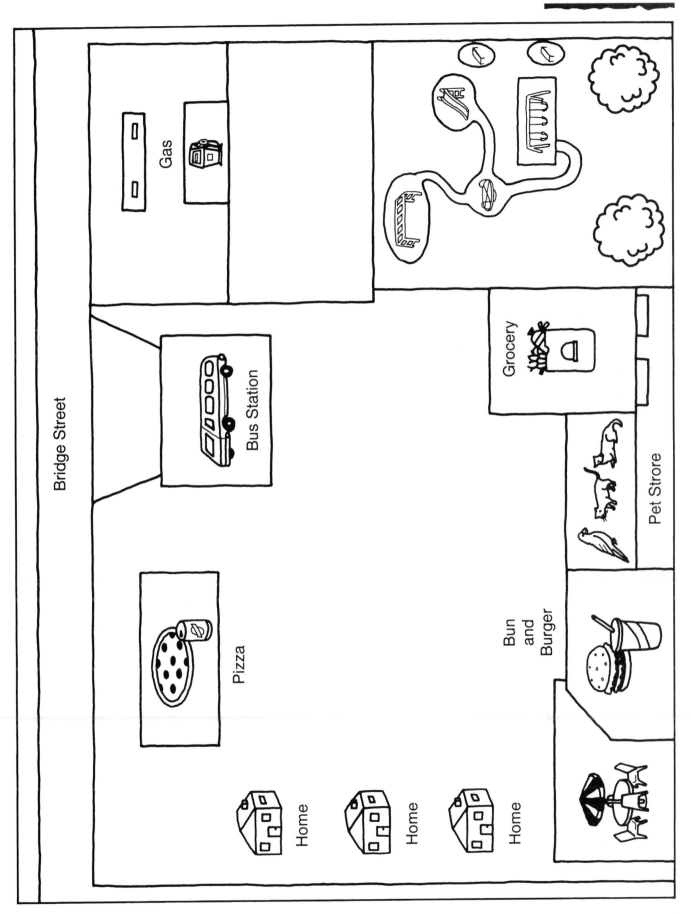

Bridge Street

Gas

Bus Station

Pizza

Home

Home

Home

Grocery

Pet Strore

Bun
and
Burger

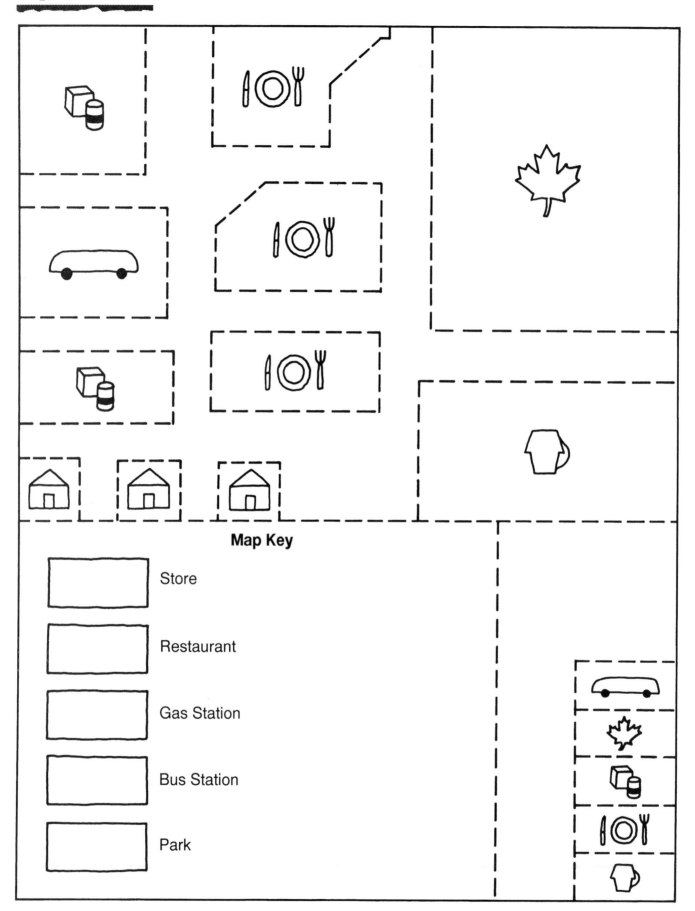

Map Key

Store

Restaurant

Gas Station

Bus Station

Park

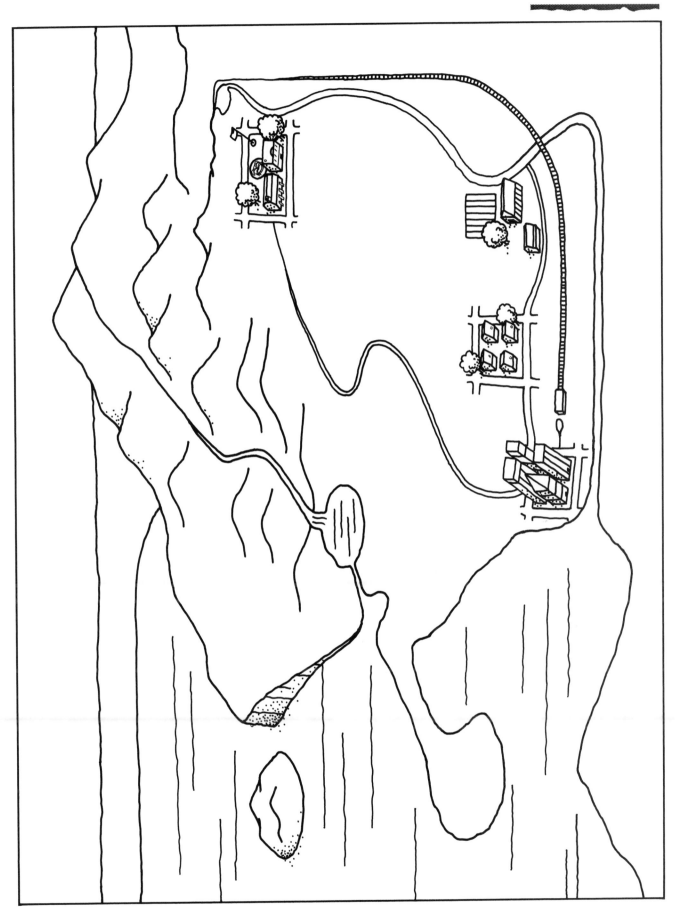

Geo-Bingo

Geo-Bingo

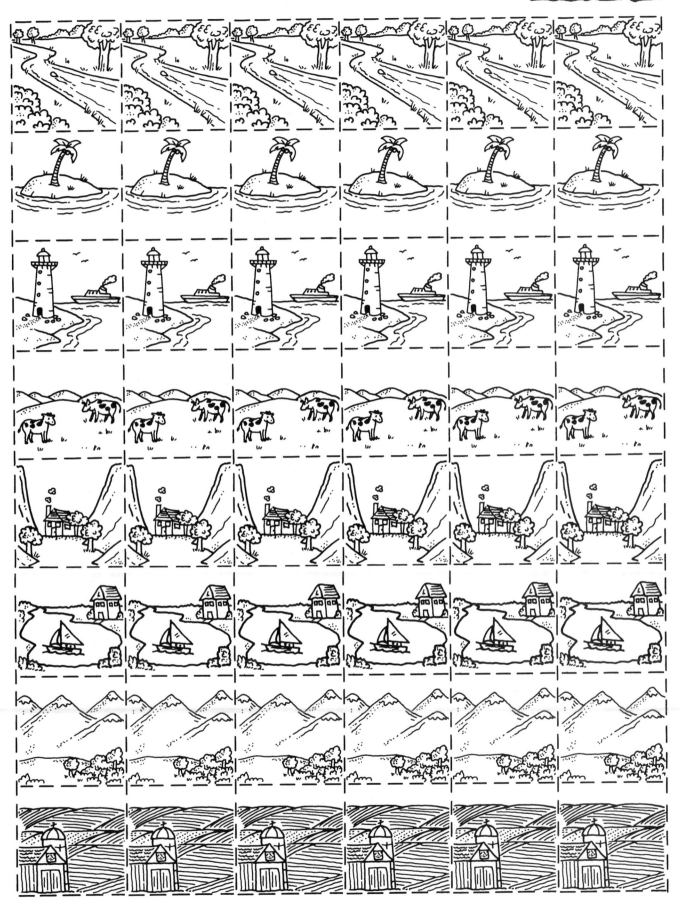

Very frigid	Frigid	Cold
Cool	Warm	Hot
Very hot	Very frigid	Frigid
Cold	Cool	Warm
Hot	Very hot	Cool
Warm	Cool	Warm

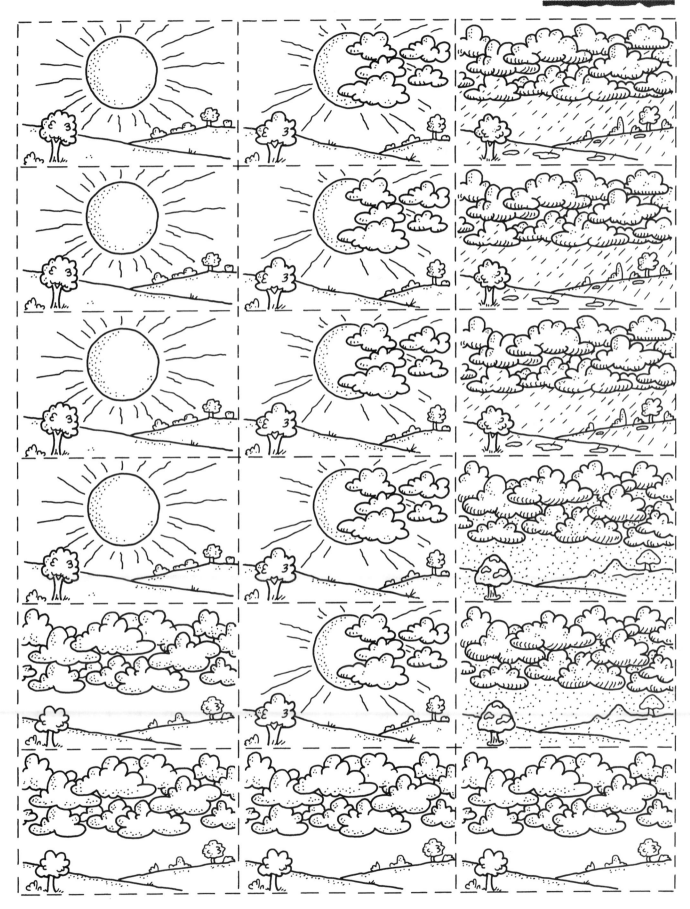

Bar Graph of _____ 's temperature for the month of _____ .

	Very frigid	Frigid	Cold	Cool	Warm	Hot	Very hot
18 days							
17 days							
16 days							
15 days							
14 days							
13 days							
12 days							
11 days							
10 days							
9 days							
8 days							
7 days							
6 days							
5 days							
4 days							
3 days							
2 days							
1 day							

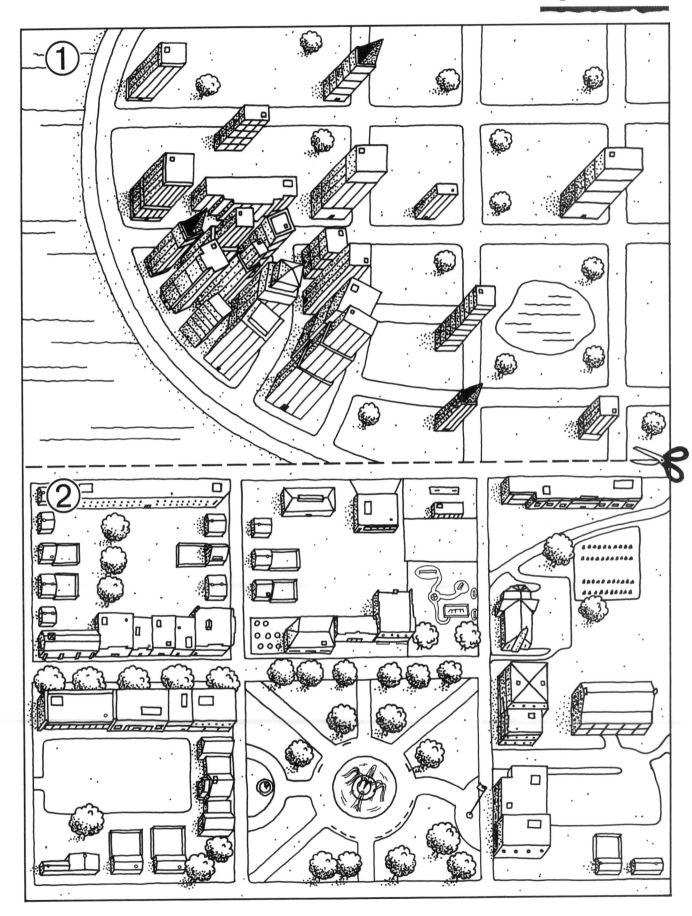

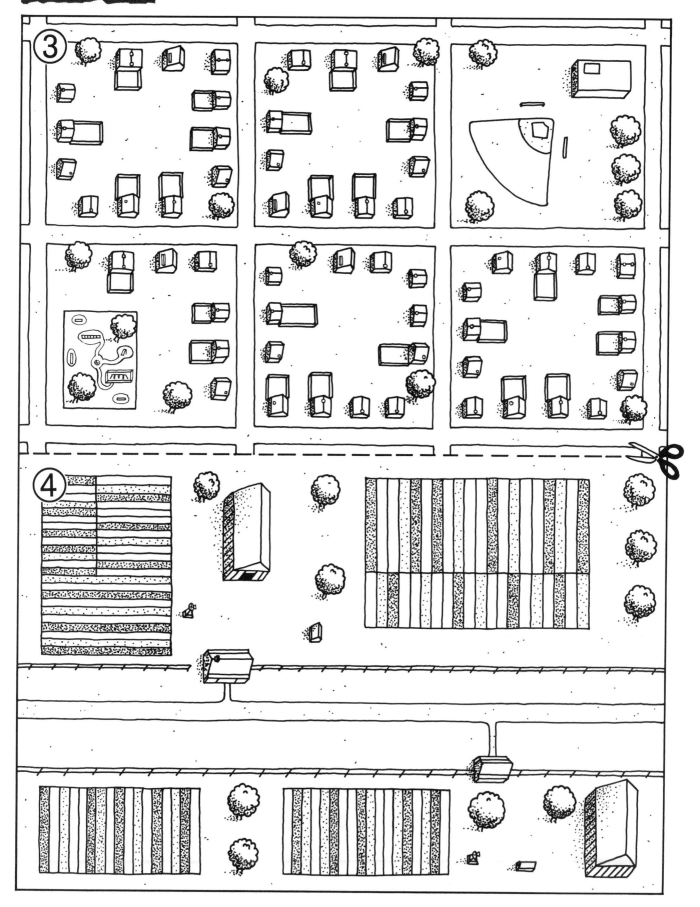

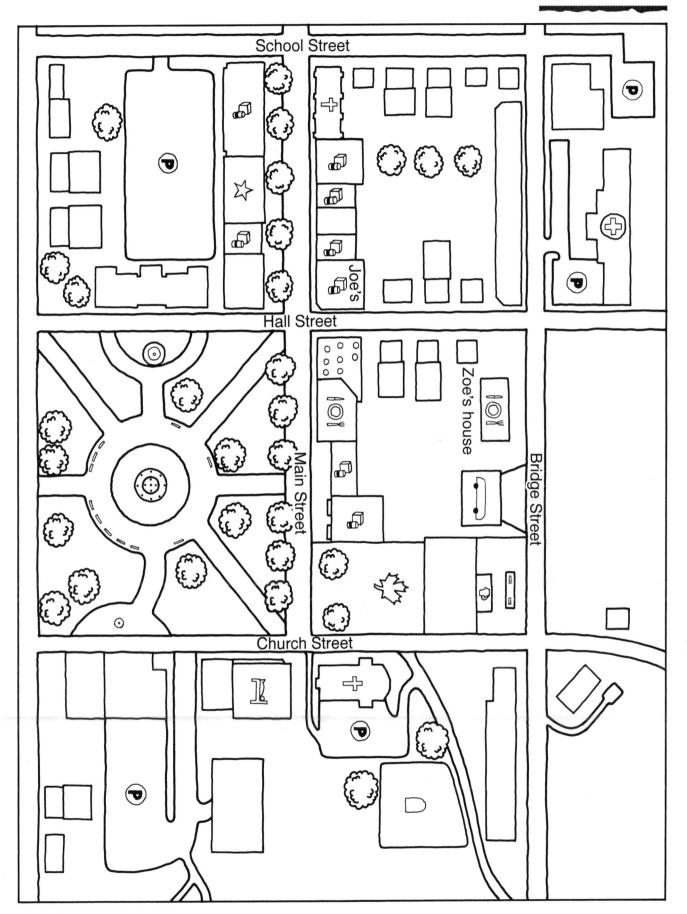

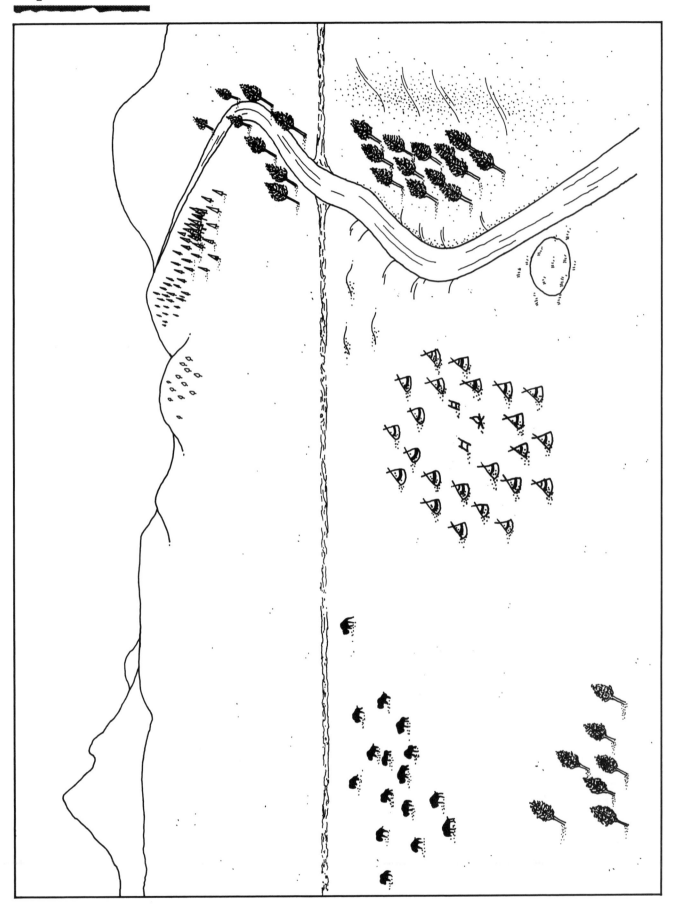

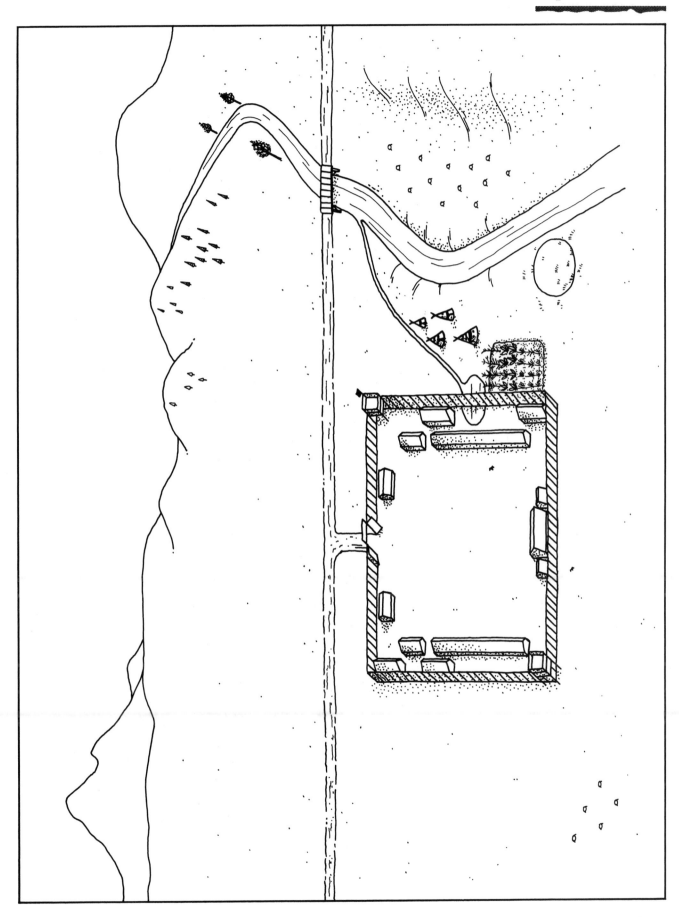

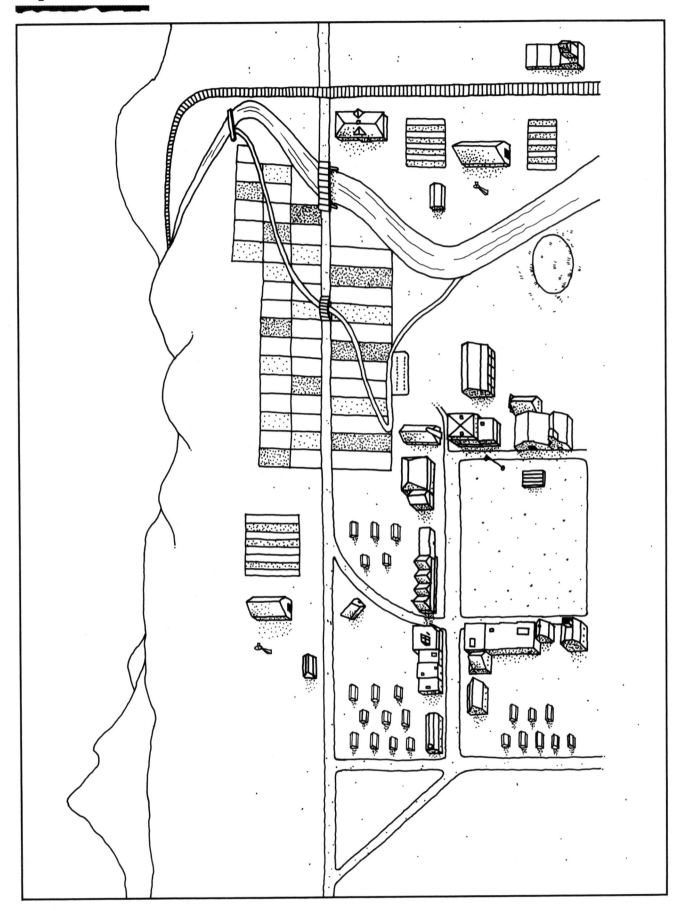

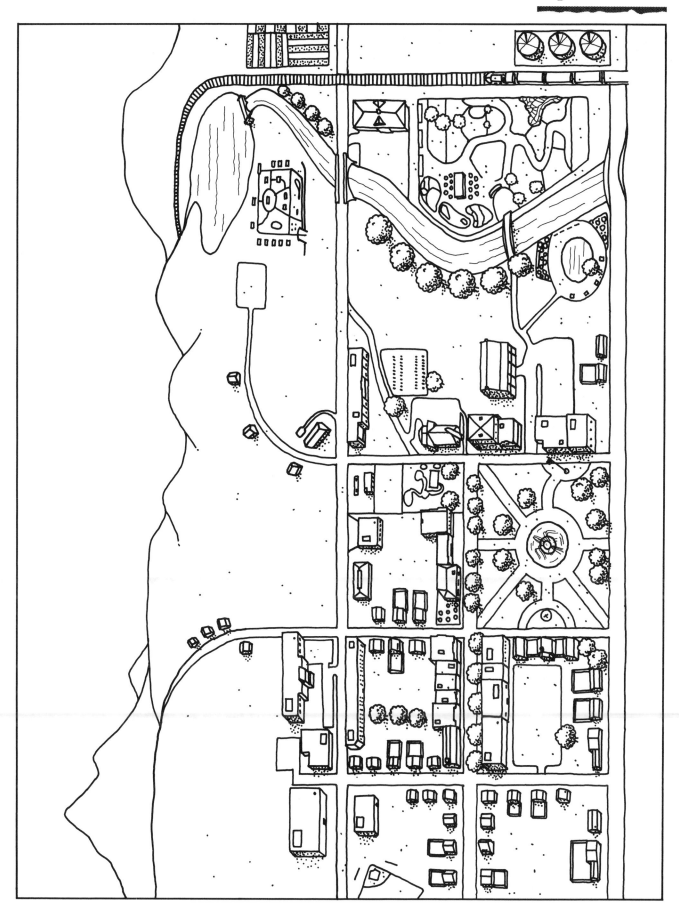

Community Center

Bike path to the fairgrounds

Park

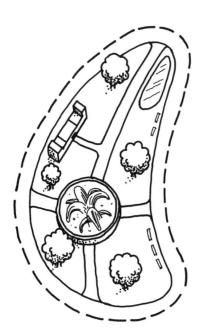

Aquarium

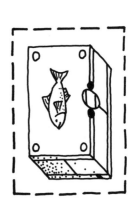

Playground

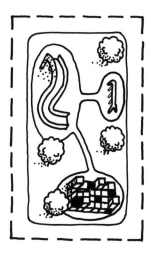

Recycling Center

Children's Museum

Community Garden

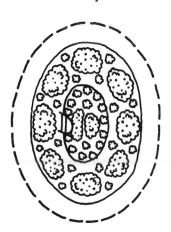

Dear Caregivers,

Did you know that you have a young geographer in your house? That is what the children in our class are learning to be. With the help of a program called **Hands-On Geography**, we are looking at the world with geographer's eyes.

Like all geographers, our class is studying places—the land and water, the climate, the plants, animals and people who make a place what it is. Sometimes we will look at all of these in a make-believe place called Geotown.

We will be using posters, pictures, models, and lots of maps to explore geography. Maps are a geographer's most important tool. Try to share with your child as many maps as you can. Let your young geographer help you whenever you read a map.

We will be making models and maps of local places. From time to time I will send home a letter asking for supplies for these projects. In addition, our class would be very grateful for any maps that you can give to our Geography Center.

Thank you for helping!

Sincerely,

Dear Caregivers:

Our class needs the following supplies to complete a geography project:

If you can supply any of the above objects, your cooperation will be appreciated. Thanks for helping to make this project a success.

Sincerely,

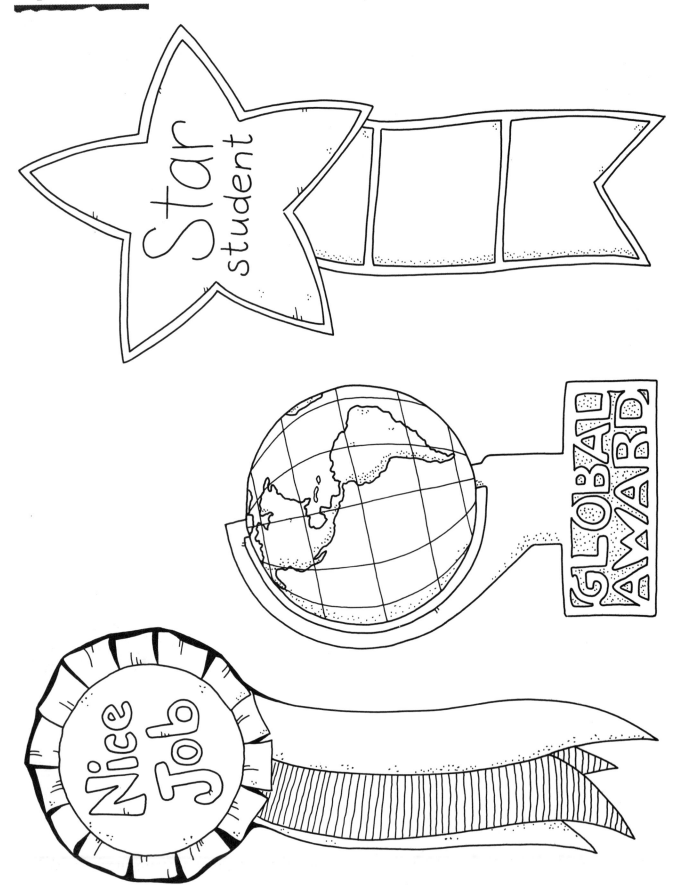

Star student

GLOBAL AWARD

Nice Job

This is to Certify that

has completed SCHOLASTIC'S study of
Hands-On Geography
and is now an official Young Geographer.